David Holzman's Diary

David Holzman's Diary

A SCREENPLAY BY
L.M. Kit Carson

FROM A FILM BY
Jim McBride

FARRAR, STRAUS AND GIROUX
NEW YORK

Published simultaneously in Canada by
Doubleday Canada, Ltd., Toronto

Printed in the United States of America

FIRST AMERICAN PRINTING, 1970

Designed by Betty Crumley

To my parents
and to R.E.A. III

1. $\triangle E$ times $\triangle t \approx h$

   —Werner Heisenberg, *The Principle of Indeterminancy*, 1927

   In other words, starting from the core of what is Real (the Basic Facts: $\triangle E$ or position, and $\triangle t$ or momentum), scientifically there is no Truth only Half-Certainty—the wormy sign ($\approx$) in this equation means "approximately" equal: that undoes it, and It.

2. 1960 Godard, *Le Petit Soldat:* "Photography is Truth, and cinema is Truth-24-times-a-second."

3. About three years ago, late winter 1967, Jim McBride and I went into a coffee shop on West 45th Street off Broadway.

4. About three years ago, late winter 1967, Jim McBride and I sat in a coffee shop on West 45th Street off Broadway. Jim was eating, as usual, a cheeseburger.

   At that time we were researching a book on *cinéma-vérité* for the New York Museum of Modern Art: *The Truth on Film*. We had just taped three- and six-hour interviews with Richard Leacock, the Maysles Brothers, Andy Warhol, D. A. Pennebaker, Andrew Noren, other cinéma-veritistes—all of them stumbling around the basic (endless) question in c-v, or filming-the-Real: *Can* you get It, the Real, the Truth, on film?

   (From this question fell all the others: What is the Real once you get It on film? Still Real? Your Responsibility to Integrity of Real before Camera—i.e., how close can you frame into subject without violating? etc. Responsibility to Integrity of Camera before Real—i.e., how much can you rip off subject to get the unmasking you need within the three-minute, ten-minute load of film? etc.)

Andrew Noren's interview cut deepest for us into the blubber about *cinéma-vérité:* there's only one truthmovie, *cinéma-vérité,* a man can make, he said, that's the movie of himself—just turn the camera directly on his own life: "Me." (And Noren made movies just like this, confronting himself at random hours: the camera squatting on its tripod coldly grinding along watching Andrew and his girlfriend drink coffee, fuck, etc.—and in one remarkable shot when the screws on the camera base are loose, the camera at last seems to be unable to watch any more and very slowly turns away from Andrew and his girlfriend in a bathtub: v-e-r-y s-l-o-w-l-y t-u-r-n-s to look at the sunshiny paisley curtain flapping in and out a window—until Noren notices, grabs the camera and jerks it around to face him again.)

This un-camera-shy Noren—in America, where most filmmakers either fear or worship the camera—this Noren who unscrewed the lens from the camera and pushed his fingers into the guts of the camera while it was running, he was on to something. We went back to argue with him and interview twice more. McBride especially wanted to re-do the tapes—you see, the year before, Jim had shot an uncompleted fictional movie about an obsessive moviemaker, like Noren, who keeps a film diary. And when Jim talked to Noren now, Noren kept kicking Jim's imagination in the ass.

5. About three years ago, late winter 1967: McBride, eating his usual cheeseburger, handed me an outline he'd written for a movie about a filmmaker named David (no last name): a sane man and loser like most, who'd finally lost his life. "My life . . . haunts me," Jim wrote David as saying: "My life . . . haunts me." To stop This, David starts filming and taping the days and nights of his existence—he figures to get his life down on plastic; then It can't get away any more.

David assumed here: you get The Real, The Fact, The Truth on film. Film, after all, started 1877 with Muybridge trotting that horse past the row of cameras to get on-film-proof that the full-trotting horse lifts all four feet off the ground at once—proof! Gov. Leland Stanford of California won his bet about the horse's hoofs using the Muybridge photo-series as proof, The Real, no doubt about it. Film is Real Light/ Real Time/ Real Space/ Real Motion/ Real Sound/ Bad Color but—that's The Real stuff, Film is Real; yes.

McBride finished his cheeseburger, said he'd now enough money to try and make the film-diary movie again. "Be a great movie," I said, starting to suggest some actors for David. McBride suggested me.

6. "I want the facts, ma'am. Just the Facts. That's all."
—Jack Webb, age 32–49 on TV
Dragnet, 1952–59 & 67–70

7. "The Facts are nothing, sir!"
    —Norman Mailer, age 47, defense
    witness in the Chicago–7 con-
    spiracy trial, 1970

8. As John Kennedy's brains explode in the millisecond
   between frames 312 and 313, Porky Pig as Jack Ruby
   pops out of the bull's-eye—stuttering like a fool—and
   (sweeping his white-gloved, three-fingered gun across
   the TV screen) he points to the "Real" Paul McCart-
   ney in Us: Richard M. Nixon (who flashes Porky a
   last uncomprehending glare of recognition).

   It's all there, the Facts right on frames 312 through
   316 of Mr. Abraham Zapruder's 8 mm. *cinéma-vérité*
   truthmovie. Have you seen It all?

9. *Q. Most of the people who see* David Holzman's Diary
   *are fooled into believing it. In fact, at the San Fran-
   cisco Film Festival, when the credits appeared at the
   end of the movie, the disappointed audience booed
   because what they thought Real turned out to be just
   a movie. Do you want* DHD *aesthetically to fake
   people out?*

   A. Someone asks this question every time. There are
   several answers.

   FIRST

   All art's a decoy. Not Real. Not Fact. Not The Truth;
   but lures you to The Real, The Truth. Obvious: you
   don't sit in a painting of a chair (not Real); you keep
   your distance, and maybe think about (The Real)
   Mr. Chair.

But a movie, motion-picture-with-sound, apparently is Real: the little kangaroo you see hopping across in front of Robert Mitchum in *The Sundowners*—that's Kangaroo in person, Real—no statue, no word; but a kangaroo. The movie medium holds The Real for decoy: a Real tree for a Real tree—it's a Real-decoy, yes. But still every movie ever made's a fake-out.

SECOND

However, from the beginning, The Real and *David Holzman's Diary* began to rush together, mix, twist, join more than usual for a movie.

Here: we had to shoot the movie in five days around Easter 1967 (no money for any more footage: $2,500 was the budget; and I had to return to school in Texas after the Easter weekend); so time pressure and the need to make every 28¢-foot of film good drove McBride, Mike Wadleigh the cinematographer, and me like maniacs—we all had to *become* David Holzman and never slip out of David or we'd lose the movie. For example, Wadleigh, interviewing the Thunderbird lady; I choked and couldn't say a word, altogether stunned by the woman (and she was driving off), but Wadleigh took over the questions—and he improvised perfectly as David; the switch from me to Wadleigh off-camera goes unnoticed by audiences. For example, I began to live like David Holzman: sleeping alone in the apartment with the camera equipment, not eating—after a few days I lost a girlfriend of two years (like David did) because she began to hate the moviemaking (like David's movie-girl, she exited on a subway late one night, her last line: "You're crazy").

Then: this was intense concentration; but not closed concentration, so The Real could break into what we were doing very easily. This wasn't a tight tiny fiction movie-world we tried to hold together inside the frame, cutting off the real world. (We didn't chase pigs out of the barnyard because they were too piggy for a movie, as they did in Cuernevaca on *Butch Cassidy*.)

"For me, the idea in filming is just to keep looking," Richard Leacock said in his interview. "Don't go after only what you've set up and that's all. Because if you don't keep open, you'll miss something every time. And you'll never see it again." (And we re-played these interview tapes over and over during that time, studying and editing them.) So we kept looking, as in *cinéma-vérité*, for whatever the moment might turn up, to grab the chance, the unrepeatable: Wadleigh buys a new fish-eye lens, we tape it on the camera and invent a scene for it; McBride wants a sequence where an old man collapses on the sidewalk; before we can stage this, some kids mug a bum and we shoot that instead. We kept open: all of a sudden we were mucking with The Real; and The Real mucked right along with us.

THIRD

"Truth and Life merge," Jim McBride always steps

up to the microphone and says in answer to this question. And smiles. And that's all.

10. *A year later, walking out after a* Diary *screening, Pennebaker said to me (funny smile): "You killed cinéma-vérité. No more truthmovies."*

No. Truthmovies are just beginning.

L. M. Kit Carson

Eclipse Day
March 7, 1970
Irving, Texas

CREDITS

CINEMATOGRAPHY: *Michael Wadleigh*
FILMMAKER: *Jim McBride*

CAST

DAVID HOLZMAN: *L. M. Kit Carson*
PENNY WOHL: *Eileen Dietz*
SANDRA, THE GIRL ACROSS THE STREET: *Louise Levine*
PEPE: *Lorenzo Mans*
THE GIRL ON THE SUBWAY: *Fern McBride*
SANDRA'S BOYFRIEND: *Michael Levine*
MAX, PENNY'S AGENT: *Bob Lesser*
THE COP: *Jack Baran*
THUNDERBIRD LADY: *Herself*

David Holzman's Diary

DAVID HOLZMAN taps the microphone five times in the dark.

Fade-up:

DAVID stands in a mirrored alcove, his camera on his shoulder.

> DAVID
>
> (*Voice gradually gets louder.*) Test, test, test, test. (*Tap, tap, tap, tap, tap.*)

He's shooting a picture of himself in one of the full-length mirrors.

> DAVID
>
> Test. (*Tap.*) Test. Okay. This is the story, this is a very important . . .

A few people pass behind him.

He pans around the alcove, swiveling quickly to catch his image in the closed-circuit Sony TV that now faces him.

DAVID

This is a fairy tale.

Now he slowly steps out of the frame in the Sony TV.
Fade to black.

DAVID

This—

Fade-up:

DAVID slowly steps sideways, shooting a picture of himself in a horizontal mirror in his apartment.

4

DAVID

Please pay attention.

Cut to black.

Cut to:

DAVID's face, out of focus.

DAVID

You've had your chance.

DAVID's face comes into focus, grinning crazily.

DAVID

You've had your chance, lad. It's now time to
stop your laboring, stop-your-laboring-in-vain.
Bring your life into focus. That's right.

He bobs up, twisting the exposure gauge on the camera
so that the screen now blacks out from underexposure.

Black.

And expose yourself. Yeah: Expose Yourself—

DAVID readjusts the exposure, correcting it, and zooms the picture back away from his face so that now one side of his room is included (behind him) in the frame.

DAVID

To yourself.

DAVID sticks out his tongue.

DAVID

Yur fuckin' self.

DAVID pulls back from the camera, flops in a low chair facing the camera. He sits in front of a simple editing table, on which are film cans, a viewscope, and a Nagra tape recorder. Two reel winders are bolted to the table. The wall behind the table is covered with film posters, stills from Godard's *Contempt, A Married Woman,* a photograph of Richard Leacock and D. A. Pennebaker, and a magazine page photo of Richard Roud, the film critic (which DAVID has hung upside down in disfavor). A mirror is centered over the table and in it the camera and tripod are reflected. DAVID sits back tensely in the chair, staring at the tape going around on the Nagra, knuckles covering his mouth.

DAVID

Urm. Shit.

Suddenly he gets up, goes past the camera out of the frame, clicking off the camera (we see this in the mirror) as he passes.

Black.

DAVID turns the camera back on; reenters the frame; flops back down at the editing table.

DAVID

Toot. This is. Okay. This is July 14, 1967. This is serious.

He reaches over and fiddles with the Nagra sound control.

DAVID

This is—serious, ss—

He's still uncomfortable, speaks without looking up at

the camera. He fiddles with the Nagra's sound again; continues to talk without meeting the camera's eye: looks down at his legs, up at the ceiling.

> DAVID
>
> Last week I lost my job. That's too bad—it's a, not such a great job—but it was the only job I had. This morning, however, I got a reclassification from the draft board: A-1. Perfectly American.

Suddenly DAVID twists, throws his arm over the back of his chair, sets his chin against his hand, stares into the camera. He stops talking, looks into the camera a moment. Then he reaches behind him, picks up a pasteboard cup of coffee from the editing table, and drinks from it.

> DAVID
>
> So now I'm gonna do something that's been on my mind for a long time. (*Swallows coffee, pauses.*)

Now he's talking again—looking at and squeezing the coffee cup in his hands, tapping it lightly.

> DAVID
>
> Objects, People, Events seem to speak to me. They seem to carry some meaning that I can't quite get.

He looks up at the camera warily.

> DAVID
>
> My life.

He raises his hand, then repeats this gesture mock-melodramatically.

"My Life." My life, though ordinary enough, seems to haunt me—in uncommon ways. It seems to come to me—from somewhere else. Someone. And I've been trying to understand it; but it seems that I can't get it.

He sets the coffee cup back on the table, picks up a small spool of film, leans forward toward the camera.

DAVID

So: the noted French wit, Jean-Luc Godard—

He checks the wall behind him, leans far back in his chair, points to a magazine photo of Godard directly behind him.

DAVID

—said: "What is film? Film is Truth-twenty-four-times-a-second."

He nods smartly, exaggerating his point a bit.

DAVID

So I thought that if I put it all down on film, and I put my thumb on it and I run it back and forth . . .

He stretches the spool of film out, displays it between his two hands held above his head. He lets one end of the film go; it bounces up against his other hand like a snake. He grabs the film, squeezes it hard. He stretches the film out again, twists it, looks at it. He rolls the film back up in his fingers.

DAVID

And I stop it when I want to, then I got everything. I got it all. I should get it all. Hah: I *should* get it all. I should get the meaning, I should understand it.

He leans forward intently toward the camera, turning the spool of film in his fingers.

DAVID

So. This is what this is gonna be. This: I'm going to make a diary. Like the famous "Lulu's Diry." My Diry.

He glances down at the film in his hand; gets up with a mock-determined, bulldog thrust to his chin; stalks past the camera, turning it off.

DAVID

(*Sings* sotto voce) My di-ah-ry.

Cut to black.

(*Music starts.*)

Fade-up:

RADIO

Arright, you with me or agin me? Helll-lllo again. Here's my best to you.

The camera shoots out of a moving car.

A skinny Puerto Rican kid riding a *Food City* bike cart looks up into the camera as it moves past him.

Panning now.

RADIO

Good morning! How are you? (*Radio fades lower into the background.*)

The camera faces down the street; then across to the opposite side of the street, where another Puerto Rican kid stands by his *Food City* bike cart.

Cut to:

DAVID

This is my land. This is where I live: the Upper West Side; New York; West Seventy-first Street.

A small boy runs down past desolate-looking brownstones, catches up with his mother and sister carrying groceries.

(*Music: Booker T. and the M.G.'s play* Green
Onions, *a march-like, rock-organ instrumental.*)

Now the camera passes three old men standing on the
front steps of a building, one man on crutches. Two
boys pass—one jumps into the air, flapping his arms
at the camera.

Cut to:

The camera passes more brownstone fronts.

DAVID
This is the famous Kent Hotel.

The sun flashes and glints down a row of apartment
windows.

Cut to:

The camera passes an alley between two apartment
houses.

RADIO
. . . with scattered showers or thundershowers.
We've had some today already . . .

Flop-squashed mattresses and an overturned sofa lie
on the sidewalk.

RADIO
. . . it's gonna be warm today too, our high will
be . . .

An old man and a woman in heavy coats stand beside
a bleak hotel marquee bannered: Stratton Hotel 342.

DAVID
William Randolph Hearst's famous "Red House,"
which he built for Marion Davies.

The camera passes Hearst's "Red House," a real-estate agent's sign stuck to the brick. The windows are covered inside with wood slats.

Cut to:

The camera passes the Ansonia Hotel, shooting up at the demonic gargoyle face set in the entranceway arch.

DAVID
This is the famous Ansonia Hotel, where Capone and the boys used to have a *hot* time in New York.

A pigeon flaps by.

Cut to:

The camera passes The Dakota. As people trudge along beside the hotel, a boy waves.

> DAVID
>
> This is The Dakota, where—Bogart, Zachary Scott once lived.

The Dakota looks somehow heroic.

Cut to:

The camera passes apartment buildings, a man walking his dog. Some of the apartment windows reflect the buildings facing them across the street. Some of the apartment windows are smashed.

> RADIO
>
> . . . And that's Booker T. and the M.G.'s, at seven minutes before . . .

Commonplace debris litters the sidewalk. The camera stops and stands facing DAVID's apartment building.

Cut to:

The camera stands facing DAVID's apartment building. Two small boys drift past.

Camera raises, zooms in quick.

The camera isolates the four front windows of DAVID's apartment, on the top floor of the building.

> DAVID
>
> This is my apartment.

Cut to:

The camera now walks down the street (slow motion). The camera passes Mr. Weisgle, the dry-cleaner and tailor on the block, standing in front of his store with three friends.

DAVID
Mr. Weisgle, the tailor.

Mr. Weisgle and a friend wave. Mr. Weisgle eases his glasses down his nose.

DAVID

Hi.

The camera passes other shops on the street: a florist (with a wall of flower pots on the sidewalk); a grocer (with baskets of fruit stacked in his doorway).

RADIO

It's 11:25. This is Bill Edmonds with News-Brief five minutes sooner from WABC Radio. Four people have been killed tonight as rioting continued in Newark, New Jersey.

A black woman in a blond wig, carrying a large white handbag, passes the camera, her eyes downcast. The camera passes between two Puerto Rican men—one man glancing back over his shoulder at the camera as it brushes by him.

Cut to:

One of the dead is thirty-four-year-old Fred Toto . . .

The camera passes two young homosexuals striding along in step, one carrying a flight bag and pulling a laundry cart of newly clean clothes.

Cut to:

RADIO

. . . A detective who was shot in the chest by a sniper in a housing project.

The camera passes a tall, gray-haired lady in a long mink coat and white gloves walking a small bulldog.

Cut to:

RADIO

. . . Toto died two hours later in St. Michael's Hospital. Also . . .

The camera passes among a family of four Negroes (three adults and a boy), continues under a dark wooden walkway where a house is being torn down.

Cut to:

RADIO

. . . killed tonight during the sniper firing was Rufus Thompson, Jr. (age about thirty-five); Robert D. Martin (age about twenty-two); and another man, so far unidentified.

The camera passes a young pregnant black woman in a plaid overcoat standing on a door step. She scratches her nose sluggishly, watches the camera walk by.

17

Cut to:

The fire department in Newark reports dozens of fires throughout the city.

The camera passes a small black girl sitting on a low metal fence. It continues by a group of people gathered on a front step: a little Puerto Rican girl in a white dress, black man squatting in an overcoat, a tough sharp young white man in a black suit, a matronly black lady watching an empty baby walker. The black matron abruptly rises as the camera approaches; just as suddenly resits.

Cut to:

New Jersey Governor Richard Hughes has declared a state of emergency, and an overnight curfew has been imposed on Newark until six o'clock tomorrow morning.

The camera approaches another group on the sidewalk: a pretty black girl and her little sister, four neighborhood teenagers drinking beer. The four teenagers mug at the camera; a tall one wearing sunglasses reaches out and grabs the lens, shakes the camera as it walks by. Another one covers his face with his jacket.

Right now it's 71 degrees in New York, under cloudy skies. This is Bill Edmonds reporting.

The camera continues walking, passes a pair of dirty-looking little girls who look up at the camera.

Fade-out to white.

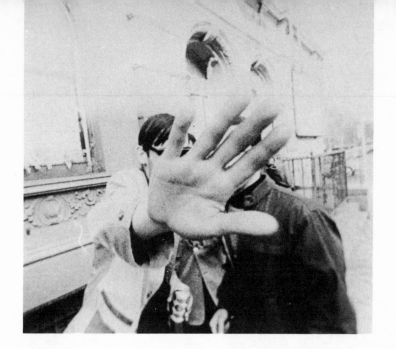

Cut to:

(*This is a series of photographs.*)

Side view (photograph) of the Eclair camera.

> DAVID
>
> I'd like you to meet my friend, my eyes, my camera: Eclair NPR.

Cut to:

Photograph demonstrating how the Eclair is loaded: the magazine being clipped into place.

> DAVID
>
> Noiseless.

Cut to:

Close-up, side photograph of the swivel viewfinder of the Eclair.

DAVID

Portable. Reflex camera.

Cut to:

Back view of Eclair camera body into which the magazine is clipped.

DAVID

She weighs about eighteen pounds.

Cut to:

Photograph of man holding the Eclair in shoulder-shooting position (the man's face is hidden by the camera).

Cut to:

Cross-section of the open film magazine. Numbers and arrows point to several places on the magazine, show how the film is to be loaded.

Cut to:

DAVID

I carry her on my shoulder.

Profile photograph of mustached man sighting through the Eclair viewfinder and twisting the exposure ring on the nose of the camera.

DAVID

Or under my arm . . .

Cut to:

Profile shot of Eclair with magazine and lens shade. Numbers and arrows point all over the body of the camera.

DAVID

. . . wherever I go.

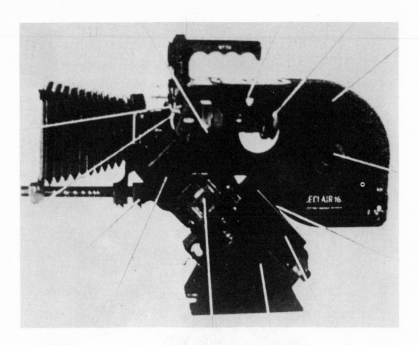

Cut to:

Close-up photograph of a finger pressing down the middle of two loops of film, loading it.

DAVID

> This is . . .

Cut to:

Close-up, side photograph of Angenieux zoom lens.

DAVID

> . . . the Angenieux, 9.5 to 95 lens . . .

Cut to:

Three-quarters front view of camera with Angenieux installed.

. . . through which Eclair takes a picture of everything twenty-four times every second.

Cut to:

Three-quarters front view of Nagra tape recorder, the Plexiglas lid flipped up and open.

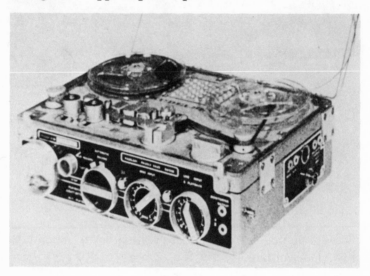

And this is Nagra, my tape recorder.

Cut to:

Close-up photograph of the 649B miniature lavalier microphone, displaying its neck cord.

And this is a lavalier mike—which I use for recording inside.

Cut to black.

When I go out on my adventures, I tie all of my friends onto me.

Cut to:

Photograph of DAVID HOLZMAN standing in front of an apartment building with his Eclair on his shoulder, his Nagra hanging on his hip. Two people stand on a balcony behind him.

DAVID

And this is how we look as we walk about: seeing and hearing, Getting It All Down.

Cut to black.

DAVID

Saturday. July 15, 1967.

Cut to:

DAVID turns on the camera, steps back, picks up a large photograph of a brunette girl's face and shoulders (her sunglasses set back on the top of her head). DAVID holds this photo up.

DAVID

This is Penny.

He shoves the photo close to the camera.

DAVID

It's Penny, see her?

He steps back, pointing off-camera; then begins pointing to the walls around his bed, on which are taped a dozen or more photographs of this same brunette girl.

DAVID

That's Penny. That's Penny. That's Penny, that's—

He sits on the edge of his bed beside his Nagra.

DAVID

All those: it's Penny. She's my girlfriend.

He taps, turns, bends the large photograph in his hands. He looks at it, lays it on the bed.

DAVID

She's a model; she does commercials occasionally.

He talks, shifts his weight uncomfortably.

DAVID

She stays here sometimes—when she can. We don't live together. She says that she can stay here when she can make it.

He looks over at the photo, picks it up again, hugs it to his chest with a smile.

DAVID

I love her, I love Penny.

He pauses a moment, leans back, rubs his nose. He shifts around, embarrassed.

DAVID

Uhhhm, we have a good time. We also have, of course, the Famous Bad Times. But: I love *her*. She's vain. She's—that's not good. But—Look: let me explain.

He stops, flops the photograph face-down on the bed, gets up and goes to the window, pulling his microphone cord after him.

DAVID

Sundays when Penny stays here—after Saturday night—she cooks breakfast for me. And one thing I demand on Sundays is bialys. So she gets them for me. I stay in bed. She gets up. She goes down to the corner and gets bialys.

He sits on the radiator, leaning back against the window, his foot orr the bed.

DAVID

Now when she leaves, I get up and go to the

window; and I watch her. And I watch and I
wait. I know she's gonna do this every Sunday.
I know she's gonna do this: I watch for her to
get to this corner over here.

He tilts his head back, looks out the window.

DAVID

And I know exactly what she's gonna do: she
steps on the corner. She stands there; and she
takes one step off onto the grate. And every Sunday
I watch and I wait to see her do that. She does
that, then she comes straight across the street.
That's touching to me. It *touches* me to see her
do that. To see her coming back across the street.

He leans stiffly back against the window board, one
hand clutching the lavalier microphone hanging around
his neck.

DAVID

I, I do love her.

He is silent a moment, staring at the camera.

DAVID

She's also dirty, sloppy.

Abruptly he lurches off the radiator seat, grabs the large
photo from the bed. He glances down at it, brings it
over to the camera.

DAVID

For instance—this picture here: she looks pretty
nice.

He shoves the photo closer and closer to the camera,
raising it in front of his face with both hands.

26

DAVID

But if you looked closer; closer. Looked closer.
Looked right there: under her chin.

He places one hand in front of the photo, points a
finger and taps under the photo girl's chin.

DAVID

You would see a surprise! You would see a little
ring of dirt.

He lowers the photo, looks down at it, lifts it again
in one hand.

DAVID

Little. Cute. Girlish dirt. Penny's Dirt.

He tucks the photo against his chest, walks back to
the bed, flips it to the bed. He walks back to the camera
waggling his hands.

DAVID

Now, she's coming in later on tonight. And you'll
see her then. For Real. Okay?

He reaches under the camera, turning it off.

Cut to black.

Cut to:

(*A series of photographs.*)

Face-and-shoulders photo of PENNY, her sunglasses back
on the top of her head, lips parted "sullenly."

RADIO

Right now the latest news.

Cut to:

PENNY's face: her chin resting "pertly" on her knuckles.

RADIO
More than three hundred Negro . . .

Cut to:

PENNY in a chrome-plated army helmet, holding up a large can of Armstrong's Epic self-polishing floor wax—her smile dimpling her cheek.

RADIO
. . . and white citizens of Newark . . .

Cut to:

PENNY's face: her brown hair falling "naturally" about her face, her mouth slightly open, her eyes "classily" seductive.

. . . have joined in a "Peace Crusade" in hopes
of ending . . .

Cut to:

PENNY's face and shoulders. She wears a jacket, sneers
"toughly."

RADIO
. . . the four days of rioting . . .

Cut to:

PENNY from the waist up in a mod frilly blouse, sailor
pants. An elbow cocked against a chimney, she leans
her head—a flirt. A block of old buildings stands behind
her.

RADIO
. . . that has taken at least eighteen lives. A U.N.
spokesman . . .

Cut to:

PENNY dancing (in profile), wearing a white sweater,
checkered skirt. A fuzzy burst of light rises in back
of her.

RADIO
. . . says the new Israel-Egyptian cease-fire . . .

Cut to:

PENNY, wrapped in a white fur coat (seemingly nude),
reclines—a little tentatively, confusedly "seductive"—
against a black backdrop.

RADIO
. . . went into effect at 6 p.m. New York Time . . .

Cut to:

PENNY, in a bikini, holds a fishnet up against her breasts. She looks "modestly seductive," really a little innocent.

RADIO
 . . . Machinist union locals in the East and West Coast say their men . . .

Cut to:

PENNY and a young man tumble nude against a dark backdrop. (This is a magazine photo. The caption reads: "The whole world vanished, and there were just the two of us alone.") PENNY is twisted hard to the side; she seems to be resisting this lovemaking.

RADIO

. . . will strike against railroads . . .

Cut to:

PENNY and a tall, young man stand in front of a tree. (This is a photograph from *True Love* magazine. The caption on the photograph reads: "I was so upset I was close to tears, but Bob wouldn't give in. 'They aren't going to be a bit of trouble,' he insisted. 'You'll see . . .'") The normalness of the young man is sinister.

RADIO

. . . at 6 a.m. tomorrow local time.

Cut to:

PENNY stands nude, brushing her fingernails, smiling to herself.

RADIO

Pentagon sources says U. S. Forces in Vietnam . . .

(*End of photo series.*)

Cut to:

Telephoto shot: PENNY (carrying a model's bag and photograph portfolio) comes around the corner opposite DAVID's house, walks a ways down the sidewalk. She glances around, steps into the street, crossing toward the camera between cars.

RADIO

. . . will probably be strengthened by at least 80,000 men in the next year. The WABC midtown temperature: 75 degrees. More news at eight on Dateline Show with Jerry Stevens.

Cut to:

PENNY, wearing DAVID's striped shirt and underwear with large stars and stripes, washes dishes in DAVID's small kitchen. Her hair is tied in two "cute" small pigtails with big loose bows. DAVID's shadow, camera on his shoulder, moves a little toward her.

> DAVID
>
> Penny. Penny, honey.

> PENNY
>
> What.

> DAVID
>
> Come in the other room. I want you to do something for me.

PENNY turns off the faucet with a knock, sets down a pan noisily, steps past the camera out of the kitchen, wiping her hands on the shirt.

> DAVID
>
> Thank you.

PENNY goes down a small hallway, into DAVID's editing room/bedroom. The camera follows her very closely—hovering at the back of her head.

> DAVID
>
> Okay. Go over to the white table; pick up that camera over there; take a picture of me.

The camera pulls back into a fuller room shot.

She stops a moment, then goes over to the white table, picks up a 35 mm. still-camera.

> DAVID
>
> You know the button.

She starts to snap a picture of DAVID, finds the shutter isn't cocked. She cocks it, a little irritation in her face (her eyes have been down, avoiding the camera so far in this scene).

Cut to:

(*Quick cut.*) DAVID stands in front of his apartment-windows: camera on shoulder, recorder on his hip. (This is the photo that PENNY just snapped.) His head is tilted back a bit as he adjusts the exposure on his camera.

DAVID
Thank you.

Cut to:

PENNY sets the 35 mm. still-camera back on the white table, wrapping the neck straps clumsily around it.

RADIO
(*Music starts: the Spencer Davis Group plays* I'm a Man, *a hard-driving rock song.*)

She turns (lifting her shoulder defensively), moves away from DAVID. She walks uncomfortably and aimlessly for a few steps (still keeping her face turned from the camera), brushing her hair tensely off her forehead with one hand. Now she lifts both hands to her forehead—for a split second she almost hides her eyes—then brings both hands down past her ears, brushing her hair back, pulling it down and out. She stops and sits at DAVID's editing table—bringing her feet up into the chair with her, tucking her thighs against her chest, her mouth to her knee like a fetus. Her fists are clenched. But now she opens one hand and lays her mouth against it; opens the other hand and attentively picks at the toes of one of her feet.

PENNY
Dav-vid.

The camera moves closer for a moment.

Now she lifts her head, props her temple on the fingers of one hand—still picking at her toes—her eyes still averted from the camera. (She is posing, but the poses are not enough defense. She is forced by DAVID's camera into an angry degree of self-consciousness.)

DAVID
Yeah? Yes.

The camera squats a little below her, facing her.

She brushes the hair off her forehead, her eyes now almost closed.

The camera moves almost directly above her.

PENNY feels the camera is watching her pick her toes: she covers her feet with both hands.

PENNY
David, put it away.

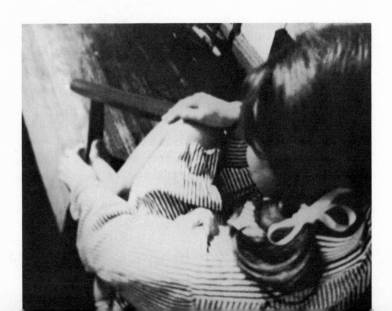

The camera moves around to close in front of her.

PENNY
DAVID

Ignore it. Ignore the camera, Penny. Forget it.

PENNY shifts her legs, turning her body away from the camera's new position as much as the chair will allow. She reaches a hand up and pulls on her upper lip—shifts farther from the camera—gnawing and sucking on her knuckles.

The camera moves up and closer to her face.

PENNY
David, I'm not dressed.

PENNY pulls her hand into her hair, then brings it back to press against her mouth.

The camera zooms slowly tighter into her face.

DAVID
Penny, the camera is your friend.

Abruptly, PENNY gets up—brushes past the camera, halts at the white table (back to the camera a moment, pulling at her forehead hair).

Penny, the camera's been here all night.

The camera moves a little behind her, catches up with her.

Suddenly she moves again, paces to the hallway, biting her thumb.

The camera trails her.

Then she turns back, walks uncertainly to the editing table, sits against it.

The camera moves in on her.

She sucks her bottom lip, turns her face away.

The camera moves below her, shooting up.

PENNY swallows. On the wall behind her, a large old poster (a painting of Cary Grant thrusting his chin against Joan Fontaine's cheek) advertises Hitchcock's *Suspicion*.

PENNY
David. If you don't put that thing away, I'm leaving.

The camera moves closer and above her, pulls back a bit.

The image washes out gray for a moment, then returns full strength. Now number perforations—formations of small white spots—pass across the image. PENNY brushes past the camera, heading for the hallway.

The camera trails her.

The image washes out for a split second, returns. PENNY reaches down, grabs her shoes—the image washes completely out to white.

(*Sound:* I'm a Man *continues on the radio, clothes hangers clatter to the floor.*)

The hand-lettered print name passes quickly.

Cut to black.

Fade-up:

(*Sound: Radio plays the last long piano chord of the Beatles'* A Day in the Life.)

Telephoto shot: Night. Two apartment windows, matchstick bamboo blinds rolled up part way in them. Sparse wrought-iron grilles raise half way up in each window. The ceiling, with its triune bare-bulb light fixture, is all that can be seen of the room inside.

> DAVID
>
> This is West Seventy-first Street, 8:30. Life Goes On. That is apartment 5-E in the building across from where I'm shooting. It's one floor above from where I'm shooting.

A thin girl in a bathrobe, her hair wrapped in a towel, walks into sight in one window. She squats and turns on the unseen TV set, rises, rubs her hair while she watches the TV. She rubs the water back from her forehead.

> DAVID
>
> It's very ordinary. Belongs to that girl that just came in and turned on the television set—Very

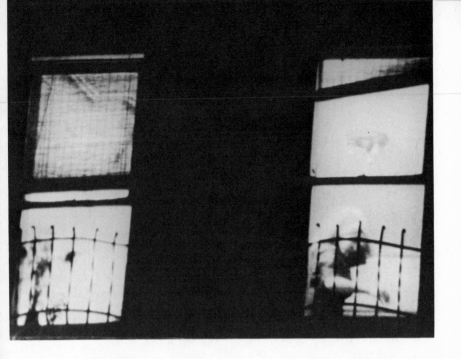

Ordinary Girl. Let's see: it's 8:30—she probably just turned on *The Life of Emile Zola* with, starring Paul Muni. Every Sunday night she washes her hair and watches whatever show happens to be on television. Aum, she moved in there about—

Suddenly the girl throws her head forward. This flings her hair in front of her.

DAVID

That's a thing about her. She's not just ordinary, not *only* ordinary. The fact that—well: the way she throws her hair back, the fact that it's long . . .

She squats to change the TV channel.

DAVID

Something— Now. She's changing the set now. She's probably watching Ed Sullivan. There's something a little more than ordinary about the girl.

Now she turns the towel around her hair, wrapping it into a cylinder, bending forward from the waist.

> DAVID
> More a little, a little more aware. A little more sensual.

She rises and walks back out of sight.

> DAVID
> It's the same thing with those matchstick bamboo curtains in the window. I watched them put those up. That's when I first started watching.

She returns to adjust the TV image for a moment.

> DAVID
> By *them* I mean her boyfriend and her. She has a boyfriend: he's sort of Italian-looking and drives a Volkswagen station wagon with a hole in the top.

Now she walks back into the apartment out of sight.

> DAVID
> See, the thing is—in these ordinary enough windows they put these sort of out-of-style but *chosen* bamboo-stick blinds.

The windows stand empty.

> DAVID
> The name on her doorbell is S. Schwartz. Which is a *fit* name for her because it answers to both sides of her. The *Schwartz* being the name for her ordinary parts.

The girl returns, a cigarette in her mouth, rubbing her hair in the towel, watching TV.

> DAVID
>
> And the S. being the name for her more *mysterious* side.

She turns abruptly, crosses the room (going out of sight in one window, coming into sight in the other), picks up the telephone receiver. She leans back against a wall, starts to talk into the telephone.

> DAVID
>
> I call her "Sandra." Because she reminds me of Visconti's *Sandra*—being opaque like that.

She moves quickly back toward the unseen TV.

Cut to black.

Cut to:

Afternoon. A corner of DAVID's main room. A Nagra tape recorder sits open (running) on top of the unplugged TV. The earphones to the Nagra are on a tripod carton beside the TV. A magazine photograph of Jean-Luc Godard in a Cardin suit is taped above the TV, above a poster to a film festival. A closed window is set in the wall beside the TV. A small radiator stands below the window.

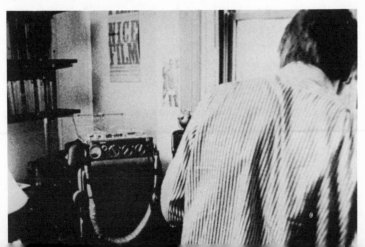

DAVID steps into the frame, walks over to the window, turns around to face the camera. He is comfortable, holding the lavalier microphone with one hand.

DAVID

This is Monday. July 17, 1967.

He sits on the window radiator, talks calmly with both hands holding the lavalier now.

DAVID

Yesterday I called Penny. We had a long telephone conversation, and we made up.

He props one shoulder back against the window edge, starting to smile a little. Embarrassed now, he looks at the wall, glances up in the direction of the ceiling.

DAVID

She was pretty upset about what happened the other night. But I promised not to ever do it again; and that made her happy.

Now he looks back toward the camera.

DAVID

I spent all day yesterday with her, that's why there's no footage on Sunday.

He pauses: lowers his head, scratches his nose, pulls his hair back off his forehead, props a hand against the window.

DAVID

I understand Penny's objections.

Now he picks up the Nagra earphones, dangles them in his hand.

I don't. Well, like, I know the difference between this kind of shooting and fashion shooting—that's simple.

He looks up: opens his hand, lets the earphone hang by his thumb, points a forefinger. He swings the earphones, waggles his fingers.

DAVID

I'm not asking her to do anything. But. All I want is herself. I don't quite *get* her "sense of privacy."

He gets up: places the earphone back on the tripod carton, paces up to the camera and back to the window— looking at the floor, moving his forearm and hand stiffly as he talks, a little angry and embarrassed.

DAVID

She shoots eight hours a day sometimes. And she's overjoyed! She's Radiant—with all that bread. But.

He looks at the camera, pulls his hair back from his forehead, grabbing and holding it back for a moment, while he talks.

DAVID

I, I don't see how I can a shoot a picture of my life without Penny being in it.

Then he looks down: confused, a little hurt, swallows resignedly.

DAVID

But: I'll let her be.

He steps toward the camera: leaning down, facing into the lens, his hair pulled tightly against the back of his head. He looks into the camera. Bemused now, he turns back to his tape recorder, starts to turn it off; stops; returns to turn off the camera first.

DAVID

It's. It's. All right. She's happy. Then I'll do what she wants.

He doesn't hit the camera turn-off button correctly. He has to reach again; now turns it off.

Cut to black.

Cut to:

PEPE, DAVID's friend (a young painter), stands before a floor-to-ceiling muraled wall. This is PEPE's kitchen: a cupboard stands at one side, newspapers stacked on top of it; a chair sits back against the mural.

PEPE takes the first puff from a cigarette, sets it down on the unseen table.

PEPE

Okay? Well: Penny is ridiculous. She's trite; she behaves melodramatically. She's just not credible.

He reaches one hand behind his back—holds it there—
talks, as he shifts from one foot to the other.

PEPE

I know you didn't set it up. I know she really
got annoyed. But I don't know—it's just— It's
not believable somehow. It looks like a very bad
actress, and a very bad script—a horrible movie,
just a horrible movie. You know, I like her.

The camera pans up a bit.

Now the mural can be seen fully, PEPE's head visible
in foreground. On one side of the mural, a man in
a light shirt, dark pants, and boots stands the full height
of the wall. He looks thoughtful, both hands folded
behind his back. Down the middle of the wall are two
capital letters: A.M. Beside the letters, a large palm
tree is silhouetted against a moon. Below the letters, the
Cuban flag waves: a white star in a blue triangle beside
five broad red-and-white stripes. Across the bottom of the
wall, a fat finger of lightning strikes at a circle containing
a man's profile. On the other side of the wall, a huge
pumpkin sits on a sand dune, and a large butterfly casts
its shadow into a square.

PEPE

It's all right, you know: if you want to live in
her bad movie. It's all right. Because some people's
lives are good movies; some people's lives are
bad movies. And Penny's life's a very bad movie.
But don't make me look at it on the screen. Please.

PEPE picks up the cigarette, takes another drag.

PEPE

The problem is that you want to make a movie

45

out of your life. All right. So you want to be in it. And you want Penny to be in it. And me to be in it. And your apartment, and my apartment. But: *I'm* an interesting character to watch; but you're not an interesting character. And Penny is certainly not an interesting character at all. I don't know. You want to make a good movie: just write a script. I'm sure you can write a better script than this. But this is not a good one. Your life is not a very good script.

He walks back to the wall, leans back against it (leaning against the legs of the mural-man).

But. Somehow, I don't think that you want to
make a good movie. What you wanna do is find
things about your life—find out the truth. There's
something that happens that you don't understand.
You want to get to the *core* of it. Well, David,
I don't think you're going to find it this way.
Because if something happens that you don't
understand—it puzzles you. You're not going to
understand it any better by freezing it all on
celluloid, and looking at it over and over again.
You know? What you have to do is try to understand it the first time.

PEPE puffs on the cigarette, taps the ash onto the floor,
pushes himself away from the wall toward the camera.

PEPE

You don't understand the basic principle: as soon
as you start filming something, whatever happens
in front of the camera is not reality any more.
It becomes part of something else.

He stands in the middle of the room, talking.

PEPE

It becomes a movie. And you stop living somehow.
And you get very self-conscious about anything
you do. "Should I put my hand here?" "Should
I put my hand here?"

He walks until he is half out of the left edge of the
camera frame, turns and walks right until he stands
in the dead middle of the frame.

PEPE

"Should I place myself this side of the frame?"

47

"Should I place myself this side of the frame?"
And your decisions stop being moral decisions,
and they become aesthetical decisions. And your
whole life stops being your life and becomes a
work of art—and a very bad work of art this
time.

He steps forward: takes a last puff from his cigarette,
crushes it out in the unseen ashtray on the unseen table,
steps back toward the mural.

PEPE

Khhhmm. I don't know. It's just very foolish to
think that there's any spontaneity in what's hap-
pening in this movie. Because you say to me:
"Look, I want to show you the film I'm doing.
And I want you to tell me what you think of
it." And then what you do?

He glances at the mural; comes forward and taps the
unseen table.

PEPE

You place me in front of the mural. You make
me move the table out of the way so you could
see it all.

The camera pans down a bit.

Now the round, empty, wooden kitchen table can be
seen partly across the bottom of the frame.

The camera pans up a bit.

PEPE

And you knew *exactly* what I was going to say.
You didn't put words in my mouth. You didn't

tell me what to say; but you knew what I was
going to say. Because you know me.

PEPE starts to walk back toward the mural-man, turns,
and walks back toward the other end of the mural.
He leans his butt against the mural.

The camera slowly zooms into PEPE.

PEPE

And I'm not going to say anything that will harm
you. I won't say any truth because I don't know
you. Just know a little bit of you.

PEPE's head now is framed beside the mural profile in
the circle. (In *close-up*, it is noticeable for the first
time that PEPE shifts his eyes around a lot as he talks.)
PEPE shifts his eyes as the zoom closes on him. He
looks away from the camera from time to time as he
talks.

PEPE

And the same way with the film. You want to
put in it a little bit of David—the safe part of
David, the David that you wouldn't be afraid
to show to anybody.

The camera slowly zooms back from PEPE.

PEPE

But there's a David that you don't want to be
in the film. And that David may be the truth.

PEPE stands, his arms hanging straight down at his sides,
and for a long time turns one hand only (wrist and
fingers) as he talks.

PEPE

And that's what you should try to put into the

49

film. If you don't dare face yourself other ways—
confess things to the camera. I don't know. Say,
say the things that you're most ashamed of. Things
that you don't want to remember. Things that
you don't want anybody to know. Maybe, maybe
that way there'll be some truth.

Abruptly he raises both hands, palms outward, then drops
them.

PEPE

Or perhaps you should take off all your clothes
and stand in front of the camera for hours. And.
And not do anything. Just stand in front of the
camera. Perhaps something magical will happen—
perhaps some truth will come out. I'm not sure.

PEPE pushes himself away from the wall: sits in the
chair set against the wall, pulls at one ear.

PEPE

But, you know, one thing I'm pretty sure of.

He rests one side of his face on his knuckles, then
he lowers his hand.

PEPE

The way you're handling this whole thing, you're
just getting half-truths. You're not getting truths,
you're just getting half-truths. And I think that's
worse than a lie. I really do.

He slumps a little in the chair, stops talking.

PEPE

Okay, that. That's all I have to say.

He notices the camera is still running: waves a hand,
leans his head forward, then settles into the chair again.

50

David, I don't want to play any games. Please: turn that off.

Cut to black.

(*This section is voice-over black.*)

DAVID

This is four. This is Tuesday morning, 4:30 a.m. About two minutes ago, Penny walked out of here. I can see her walking out of the building now. Hhht. About twenty minutes ago, I got up. And I was reading, and then I went to the john. And when I came out, I didn't go right back to bed. I stood in the hallway; and I watched Penny sleep. While I was watching her sleeping, it struck me that what I was looking at was like one of those rooms—one of those glass-enclosed rooms at the Smithsonian Institute. It was like—rooms in which everything is so perfect that— Everything is so: *perfect.*

Cut to:

Night. PENNY asleep nude—DAVID's wrinkled double bed. A small gooseneck reading lamp bends over one side of the bed. A tripod stands beside the bed near the lamp, DAVID's corduroy bush jacket draped over it. The window shades above the bed are pulled all the way down. The bed sheets and dark paisley bedspread are down in a twisted pile at the end of the bed.

DAVID

That they have to be kept. That— Because this random . . .

51

The camera (hand-held) moves around to one side of the bed.

PENNY twists over in her sleep, turns her back to the camera.

>   DAVID
> . . . particular, accidental, state is so meaningful. It's so, it's so touching. It's so *touching*.

Camera zooms slowly into PENNY.

>   DAVID
> It's so beautiful.

PENNY shifts her head and shoulders a little deeper into the pillows.

Quick lap dissolve into:

The camera stands directly above PENNY.

PENNY sleeps on her side: the smaller fingers of one hand at her lips, the other arm lying across her bust.

Camera turns and zooms into PENNY's face from above.

Camera pulls back from PENNY's face.

The camera begins to move (hand-held) back from the bed.

PENNY's back is to the camera. As it withdraws, we see the dirty soles of her feet. PENNY (still sleeping) turns onto her back: grabs one of the pillows, rolls over on her side toward the camera, tucks the pillow into her stomach. She pulls her legs up a bit into a fetus position.

The camera continues to pull back until it is all the way across the room from the bed.

Then the camera starts to lower itself (DAVID squats, holding the camera).

PENNY abruptly wakes up, shoves herself into sitting for a split second. She hurls out of bed across to the camera—her mouth wide, screaming. She grabs the camera; pushes it to one side, to the other; tries to pull it with her. Suddenly she releases it; steps back rubbing her eyes, shaking her head.

Cut to black.

Tuesday. July 18, 1967.

Cut to:

Day. DAVID sits on the edge of his bed, the Nagra running beside him. He picks up the telephone, dials a number on it. He brings a lavalier microphone up to the telephone receiver, which he places against his ear. He turns up the volume on the Nagra (repositions the lavalier), glances up at the camera, grins foolishly.

(*The phone rings twice.*)

PENNY

Hellom.

DAVID

Hello, Penny. Hello, hi.

PENNY

David? David, do you have the camera running?

His face saddens, stiffens. The lavalier slides down the telephone a little. He doesn't move, just breathes into the phone.

PENNY hangs up her phone.

DAVID lowers the phone and microphone into his lap. He doesn't move for a moment. Then he glances at the tape recorder, starts to turn it off; stops. He starts to turn the camera off; stops. He starts to turn off the tape recorder, stops; turns back to the camera—leans in to turn the camera off (frowning a little, avoiding direct eye contact with the camera).

Cut to black.

Cut to:

Telephoto shot: Day. SANDRA, DAVID'S mystery girl across the street, comes down the front steps of her apartment building carrying a small, neat garbage sack. She is dressed in a crisp dark jacket, light sweater, dark skirt— her hair cleanly held down with a dark scarf.

DAVID

Sandra: Tuesday, by day.

The camera pans with her.

She walks down the street a bit.

DAVID

I want you to watch a movement that she makes.

She drops the garbage sack in the garbage can, puts the lid on the can.

DAVID

In one of his diaries, Truffaut writes about a movement that Debbie Reynolds makes in *Singing in the Rain*.

She flicks her wrist after depositing the garbage; strides on.

DAVID

Now watch her hand: wah–*that*. Did you see the way she threw the dirt away? Yeah n-now.

Camera pans with her until the side of the window enters the frame and cuts her off from view.

Cut to black.

DAVID

Truffaut says that, in *Singing in the Rain*, Debbie Reynolds jumps over a couch and holds in her skirt as she does it.

Cut to:

Camera moving sideways (hand-held) away from a door.

SANDRA exits the door of the drugstore, walks to the corner, crosses the street.

DAVID

And this movement gives her away. Now the movement that Sandra just made and that I caught has given her away.

Camera pans (hand-held) with her, remains stationary, stops.

SANDRA walks away down the block without noticing DAVID.

DAVID

A little bit more now, by her moves. More and more, she gives herself away—to me.

Cut to black.

Cut to:

Day. A black Ford Thunderbird drives down the street toward the camera.

The camera pans with the car.

The car stops; the WOMAN driving it gives the camera the finger.

The camera (hand-held) moves at an angle up to the car.

THUNDERBIRD LADY

What are you looking for? Uranium?

The WOMAN reaches out of the car and grabs the long shotgun microphone.

THUNDERBIRD LADY

That's nice. You should put a rubber on that. You'd be right in business, baby. Put a contraceptive on that.

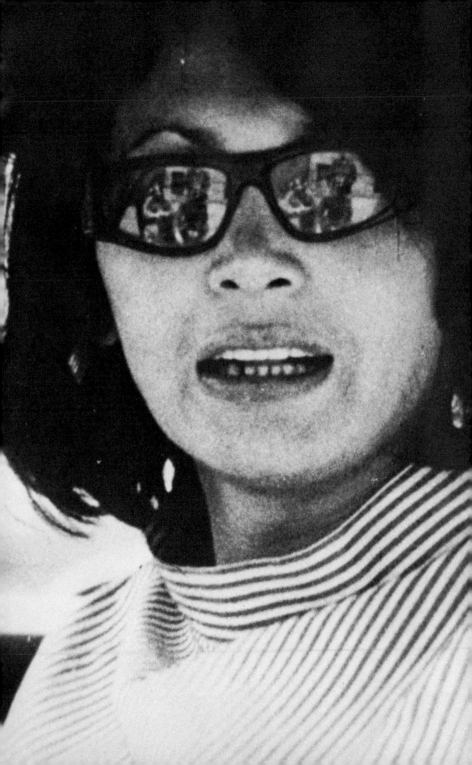

The camera moves a bit to face the WOMAN more directly.

The WOMAN reaches out, touches DAVID's leg, glances up into the camera.

> THUNDERBIRD LADY
> You got no dick. What do you wear, jockey shorts? Where's your dick, honey? What do you do, hide it or wrap it?

The camera shifts a bit more.

The woman shoves her car's gear stick into the *Park* position, rubs behind her sunglasses, jiggles her full left breast under her dress with her right hand.

> THUNDERBIRD LADY
> You want to get a look at those, baby? How's that?

She brushes some imaginary dust off her left breast with the tips of her right fingers—blows some of the dust off.

> THUNDERBIRD LADY
> You like that, baby? That's that air pollution in this city: 2.3 percent falls a day.

She smiles, looks around; leans a bit more out of the car.

Freeze-frame:

The WOMAN leaning out of the car a bit.

> DAVID
> I guess I should explain this apparition.

Cut to:

Photograph of DAVID standing in front of an apartment

building, his Eclair on his shoulder, his Nagra hanging
on his hip.

DAVID

You remember this picture that Penny took of me
with all my friends tied onto me.

Two people are on a balcony behind him.

DAVID

Well. Well, look in the back.

Cut to:

Close-up of section of photograph: the woman-in-the-
Thunderbird is one of the two people standing on the balcony. She stands smiling, her arms resting on the metal
balcony fence. A mop and a rug hang on the balcony fence
beside her.

DAVID

There: is *this* lady. She started talking that day,
and I didn't have any film in the camera.

Cut to:

Close-up of section of photograph: DAVID's face, Eclair
on his shoulder. He is touching his nose with one finger.

DAVID

And I asked her if I'd ever see her again. She
said sh-sure, she's around here all the time.

Cut to:

Same photograph: DAVID rigged up with his shooting
equipment.

DAVID

So. Tuesday: there she was. So I stopped her.
And what followed follows.

Cut to:

Camera shoots into the WOMAN's car from a low angle
(DAVID squats).

The WOMAN sits in her Thunderbird, talking to the camera.
She rests one arm on the car windowsill.

> THUNDERBIRD LADY
>
> Now listen, baby, tell me your dimensions there.
> How big are you?

> DAVID
>
> (*Laughs.*) I've forgotten.

Camera zooms a bit into the THUNDERBIRD LADY.

> THUNDERBIRD LADY
>
> You don't know how big you are? Do you think
> you have the family size, or a little more?

She raises one hand a bit, cigarette between two fingers.
She sucks in one cheek, taps the ash from her cigarette.

> DAVID
>
> Mm. A little more.

> THUNDERBIRD LADY
>
> A little more? What's it in circumference?

> DAVID
>
> I don't want to talk about it. Why don't you
> talk to me about yourself first.

She looks away.

> THUNDERBIRD LADY
>
> Look. I'm looking for big dicks—

A driver eases his taxi past the other side of her Thunderbird. The TAXI-CAB DRIVER waves his hand at her in
disgust, yells at her.

> THUNDERBIRD LADY
> Move for what??

The WOMAN electrically rolls down the window near the taxi, points at the TAXI DRIVER. She waves her hand.

> THUNDERBIRD LADY
> What's your problem??

The TAXI DRIVER gestures that she's taking up too much of the street, blocking traffic.

> THUNDERBIRD LADY
> Well, that's too bad, honey. Look how big I am;
> I need a big street.

She rolls up the window near the taxi, turns away from him. She turns back to him; he is waving his hand again.

> THUNDERBIRD LADY
> I need a big dick too.

She holds up both hands, thumbs extended, thumb tips touching. She turns away. She turns back; the TAXI DRIVER edges a little more past her. He raises one fist to his mouth. She points at him before he can bring his fist down.

> THUNDERBIRD LADY
> Yeah. You too: you look the type!

She turns away from the taxi, taps out her ash.

> TAXI DRIVER
> You look like an idiot!

She turns back to the taxi, waving one hand.

The camera shifts around a little.

THUNDERBIRD LADY
You look like a lesbian! Doesn't he?

The WOMAN leans back in her seat, points to the TAXI DRIVER while she inclines her head toward DAVID.

THUNDERBIRD LADY
Doesn't he look like a lesbian? Take a picture of him.

Camera zooms past the WOMAN into close-up on TAXI DRIVER.

DRIVER (out of focus for a moment, then into focus) smirks—looks away—looks back toward camera, grinning a little uncomfortably. He says something—looks away—sneaks a look back at the camera. The TAXI DRIVER: middle-sized, black-rimmed glasses, chunky face.

THUNDERBIRD LADY
What are you taking, baby?

DAVID
Well. We're doing a survey.

Cut to:

The WOMAN leans back, checks the Nagra hanging on DAVID's hip.

THUNDERBIRD LADY
I don't see that fucking thing twisting. I think you're full of shit.

DAVID
Do you really?

THUNDERBIRD LADY
Yeah. That's not running, is it? You're taking a survey?

64

She taps the ash from her cigarette. She leans toward the camera.

> THUNDERBIRD LADY
> Well, I'm a peniorologist. I'm taking a survey also. That's a bone specialist.

She watches a man pass behind DAVID.

> THUNDERBIRD LADY
> You look very good with that cigar, baby. Suits you.

> DAVID
> I'd still like to know why you're down here. Where do you live? How come you're down *here?*

> THUNDERBIRD LADY
> I'm just out looking for a good lay. I need a good hump today.

She puts her hand to her mouth, calls to a passer-by.

> THUNDERBIRD LADY
> This is a dirty movie—wanna be a stunt man for a stag movie?

She lays her head against her arm, looks up into the camera.

> THUNDERBIRD LADY
> What was that broad doing up in your apartment— getting layed?

Cut to:

Camera now close up to the WOMAN's face.

She rubs her hand suspiciously under her lips, points into the camera with two fingers.

65

DAVID

You tell me first: what do you do for a living?

THUNDERBIRD LADY

I do modeling. I'm a nude model.

DAVID

A nude model.

THUNDERBIRD LADY

What's this for?

DAVID

Well, do you earn enough money to buy a car like this?

She leans back into the car; sits up in the seat: bounces her breasts.

THUNDERBIRD LADY

Yeh. I earn enough. You should see me in the nude—I got lovely Happy Valleys. You'd really like 'em.

She points at the camera—notices a woman passing behind DAVID—points to the passing woman.

THUNDERBIRD LADY

Listen now. What's this for? Do you want to get into it, dearie? Make a star out a ya.

Cut to:

Camera pans quickly away from the Thunderbird.

A pair of lady's feet walk past, her long dress slapping at her ankles.

THUNDERBIRD LADY

Fill those cheeks out a little.

Camera pans quickly back to the Thunderbird.

The THUNDERBIRD LADY holds her hand against her mouth, twists her head to talk to a passer-by.

> THUNDERBIRD LADY
> *Candid Camera,* honey.

She looks back into the camera, points into it.

> THUNDERBIRD LADY
> Listen now. Let's get down to bare facts. You wanna get laid?

She leans back into the car, waggles both hands sarcastically.

> THUNDERBIRD LADY
> Never mind— Do you want to or don't you? Huh?

She licks her lips.

She picks up a pack of cigarettes, speaks over her shoulder to the little poodle in the back seat of her car.

> THUNDERBIRD LADY
> Prissy, go get that fuck. Go get him. You like my dog?

The camera pans a bit.

The little poodle hops up, pokes its head out the window. She takes a cigarette from the pack, taps it on the steering wheel. The poodle sniffs her shoulder.

> THUNDERBIRD LADY
> Listen, you want to get laid or don't you?

She lights her cigarette, shakes out the match, looks up into the camera.

67

DAVID

I think I'd rather make films.

She bends to the camera a bit, brushes her bottom lip with her finger.

THUNDERBIRD LADY

Make what?

DAVID

Films.

THUNDERBIRD LADY

Wellll. What are you: asexual? What do they call that? A-sexual, p-sexual—what they call that? A person that doesn't like both. Either. What do they call that?

Camera drops, zooms into the THUNDERBIRD LADY a bit.

DAVID

A voyeur.

THUNDERBIRD LADY

A what??

DAVID

A voyeur.

She tilts her head, takes a drag on her cigarette, turns to the camera.

THUNDERBIRD LADY

Oh, you're a "voy-yer." What's that, something new? You know, they've got some new skirts out. You know? They've got those "pilot" skirts. They go up to the cock-pit. They're beautiful.

She nods to the camera, flicks her cigarette with her thumb. She bites on her cigarette, leans forward.

Cut to:

The camera pans fast away from the Thunderbird.

THUNDERBIRD LADY

Look at her. Look at her. Look at her. That sexy look she's giving me. Behind your back.

A small, thin, middle-aged lady, a scarf around her neck, peers over her shoulder toward the camera.

The camera zooms to the middle-aged lady.

The middle-aged lady enters her apartment building shyly.

The camera pans fast back to the Thunderbird, drops a bit.

THUNDERBIRD LADY

Turn around: let me see your ass. You got a good body. Stand up. Got a good pair of thighs.

The THUNDERBIRD LADY waves, points into the camera, looks past the camera at bystanders.

The camera zooms into the THUNDERBIRD LADY a bit.

DAVID

How come you're so preoccupied with sex?

THUNDERBIRD LADY

Lookit, honey. Sex is my main course. What are you: shitting?

DAVID

What's that?

THUNDERBIRD LADY

A cock or two will never hurt anybody. And I like one-a-day. I take it like I do a vitamin pill.

69

BYSTANDER
What's for dessert?

THUNDERBIRD LADY
Hah?

BYSTANDER
What's for dessert?

The woman clicks her cheek at the camera. She holds her cigarette in her teeth, glances up at the questioning bystander, waggles her hand.

THUNDERBIRD LADY
What do I have for dessert? Ahh, that's a little too personal. I can't tell you that.

DAVID
Why do you hang around with fags then?

THUNDERBIRD LADY
Huh?

DAVID
Why do you hang around with fags then?

THUNDERBIRD LADY
'Cause I know they can't hump ya. They don't like pussy. Why do you hang out with men, I mean women? 'Cause ya know men won't hump ya. Right? So therefore you're better off with women. I hang out with fags 'cause I know they won't bother me.

DAVID
I thought you liked sex.

She shifts far back into the car. She leans forward, one arm on the windowsill.

THUNDERBIRD LADY

I do, honey. But once in a while you hafta get away from it. I'm not a launching pad. Everybody puts their missile in ya, then takes off—BOOM: it's over with.

She lays her face on her arm, reaches out the window to stroke the shotgun microphone.

THUNDERBIRD LADY

It's so big. I'm better off with that. It is.

She holds her cigarette in her mouth—takes a small puff—cocks her head at the camera.

DAVID

I like your philosophy.

THUNDERBIRD LADY

You like my philosophy. You'd like my body too, if you saw it. How old are you?

DAVID

How old do you think I am?

THUNDERBIRD LADY

Look, I'm not playing games. How old are ya?

DAVID

Mm. Twenty-six.

She nods approval to the camera, licks her lips.

THUNDERBIRD LADY

Very nice. Still got a good few humping years left. You've got a very hairy body, I bet.

(*All sound stops.*)

She looks up, talks to a bystander, smiles up at him;

71

looks away to a passing car—puts her wrist against her lip.

DAVID

Unfortunately—for her—the Street Goddess never got to find out whether I had a hairy body or not. At about this point, the tape ran out.

She reaches out for the shotgun microphone again.

DAVID

And. It was: the crowd of onlookers began to get—too big. And it was getting to be too much of a hassle. So I terminated the interview.

Cut to black.

Cut to:

3,115 TV images flash by—each lasts for one frame or 1/48th of a second. This covers an evening's television from *The Huntley-Brinkley Report* to the middle of *Bright Eyes* (The Late-Late Show with Shirley Temple).

DAVID

An evening with television. This is a record of an evening I spent watching television. This is a record of every shot on every show that I watched. Let me explain: what I wanted to do was I wanted to show you everything; but I didn't want to film excerpts. So I set the camera up in front of the set. And every time the shot changed on the set, I clicked off a frame on the camera. So: what you have in essence here— very quickly—is every image that passed through and into my head that evening. Ahhhhh.

Cut to black.

Wednesday. July 19, 1967.

Cut to:

The camera faces the doors between two subway cars.

Through the open doors the camera looks down into an almost empty, early-morning subway car.

The camera pans.

A subway poster ad: PENNY in a chrome-plated army helmet holding up a large can of Armstrong's Epic self-polishing floor wax. Some graffiti artist has changed the wax can PENNY holds up into a big spurting penis with two hairy balls. The word "Epic" on the can has been changed to the word "Prick."

Cut to black.

The camera faces a window of the subway car.

The reflection of a seated GIRL floats in the window glass.

Camera pulls back and pans across to face the real SUBWAY GIRL.

A thin old man (in dark baggy pants, a white short-sleeve shirt, white socks, dark shoes) sits several feet away from DAVID and the SUBWAY GIRL—watching both of them pointlessly.

The SUBWAY GIRL wears a short knit dress; her long, thin, wavy hair drops down below her shoulders. The GIRL has high cheekbones; carries her head up on her long neck a little like Nefertiti.

She brushes back her hair with one hand; looks away

from DAVID. She holds on to her seat tightly with both hands a moment. She places her hands on her knees, shifts away from DAVID a bit. She gets more uncomfortable, glances up at the ceiling; looks away from DAVID farther down the length of the subway car.

Lights flash past outside the windows.

She gets up (a little early for her stop), self-consciously crosses the subway car; stands by the door.

The camera pans with her, gets up.

She glances over her shoulder as the camera approaches her.

The subway stops. The door opens.

The SUBWAY GIRL gets off; walks down the subway platform.

The camera walks after the GIRL.

The GIRL walks down the dark subway platform, shoving through the metal exit gates.

The camera follows.

The GIRL walks faster, goes up one flight of subway-exit stairs, glances back toward the pursuing camera, turns the corner, goes up another flight of stairs onto the street above (again glancing back twice).

The camera follows, gets closer.

The GIRL walks to the street corner, getting farther away. She steps into the brick street.

The camera changes exposure, the image darkens slightly.

The GIRL crosses the brick street (walking down the white crossline); her wide steps pop her knit dress neatly against her nice bottom. She walks into a small triangular park, slowing down now.

The camera closes on the GIRL.

She glances back, sees the camera still after her, picks up her pace, her hair bouncing out from her head. Her white-heeled shoes flash against the dark grass.

The camera moves at an angle, cutting the GIRL off.

She glances back again, walks faster—runs a few steps— veers between some benches—heads off from the park; crosses the street, running now.

The camera zooms after her.

The GIRL reaches the opposite side of the street; starts to turn.

Cut to:

Photographic enlargement of SUBWAY GIRL's head.

She turns to the camera, her face going in and out of focus.

SUBWAY GIRL

Beat it.

Camera flash-pans away from the GIRL.

Cut to black.

Cut to:

The camera walks slowly in front of benches full of old people. (The old people sit in the sun, scarcely moving as the camera passes their faces.)

The camera passes:

A white-haired matron in a white coat, turning away. A sharp, doorknob-nosed little man in dark glasses and a snap brim hat, smirking at the camera. An old woman in half-frame glasses—arms folded on her knee—breathing through her open mouth. Two old women in dark coats half facing each other. An old woman, an old man, and their large black poodle squinting into the camera. A small man in a leather cap sitting slack-jawed. An old man in a canvas cap calmly folding his newspaper. An old woman in a dappled blouse, a raincoat, bending forward over a magazine.

The camera passes:

A blond, husky, mid-thirties woman smiling at an old little George Grosz woman—who is hiding her chin in the tall collar of her black fur coat. A hawk-nosed, curly-headed woman: her fuzzy, cream-colored coat hung around the shoulders of her low-necklined black dress, lidded eyes watching the camera. A small, practical woman: her hands fold in her lap, she stares into the camera with great composure. A very fat woman in a peasant blouse—leaning on one arm—reading a thick, paperback philosophy textbook (looking like the Mama of the Katzenjammer Kids). After a space: a small, glum woman in pointy sunglasses. Two men in overcoats and small hats raring back a bit from the camera.

The camera passes:

An empty bench space. A gaunt, elongated man in a worn-out cardigan, stretching back over the bench to spit behind it.

The camera passes:

Two little hen-like ladies turning from conversation silently to the camera. A dry little man in a Homburg, dark coat, thick glasses—opening his skeletal mouth. Three plump old ladies in dark coats, fur hats. One fortyish lady in a jag-pattern wool coat and black head scarf: putting on lipstick.

(The U.N. roll call begins softly on the sound track.)

U.N. ROLL CALL
. . . abstain. Kuwait? *Yes:* yes.

The camera passes:

A welterweight type in a canvas hat—with heavy eyebrows—resting his heavy hands on his knees. A skinny old woman in black, cringing at the camera's approach—glaring into it—covering her eyes with her hand as the camera moves on.

U.N. ROLL CALL
Laos? *Abstention:* abstain.
Lebanon? *Yes:* yes.
Lesotho? *No:* no.

The camera passes:

A bald, blind man, sightless eye-slits open to the sun (dark glasses flipped up onto his forehead). A fat little woman in a white coat, a plastic scarf. A dour little Italian man in black suit, black hat. An old lady in a knit hat, folding her newspaper. Two buxom old women

79

leaning together. A small, sad old man slumping in the bench.

U.N. ROLL CALL

Liberia? *No:* no.
Libya? *Yes:* yes.
Luxembourg? *No:* no.
Madagascar? *No:* no.
Malawi? *No:* no.
Malaysia? *Yes:* yes.
Malawi? Mali? *Oui:* yes.

The camera pulls back and passes:

Three women in sunglasses and overcoats, their hands crossed on their purses. A fortyish man, with a big Roman face, leaning out toward the camera. An old woman in sunglasses, holding packages on her lap. Two older women talking. A spectacled old man in a V-neck sweater and jacket—smiling up at DAVID, not at the camera. Two old brothers. A small, fierce old Russian woman: mouth straight, glaring at the camera. Two sharp, thin guys leaning out together: snappy hats, looking down the bench row. An old lady with sad-angled eyebrows, wearing a very wide-brimmed black hat. Two old women sitting sideways together. An old woman glancing at the camera, opening her mouth in alarm, dropping her hand. An old woman in pointy glasses, wearing costume-jewelry pins, two large necklaces.

U.N. ROLL CALL

Malta? *Not participating:* not participating.
Mauritania? *Oui:* Yes.
Mexico? *No:* no.
Mongolia? *Yes:* yes.
Morocco? *Yes:* yes.

80

Nepal? *Abstain:* abstain.
Netherlands? *Yes:* yes.
New Zealand? *No:* no.

The camera passes:

A thin old woman pitching forward—white, stringy hair falling about her forehead, her ears. A hawk-nosed old woman turning her sharp profile to the camera. A bald old man—his coat falling off his shoulders, his eyes closed—wrapping his arms across his stomach (mummy-like). A rugged little man in a heavy, vested suit (no tie). An old woman, holding her hand self-consciously at her chin.

The camera passes:

A jowlish old woman in a white coat. Two fortyish women talking, holding their hands at their breasts. Two old men in overcoats and hats, looking up at DAVID. Four little old women laughing and talking to a passer-by. A nurse-like matron (in a white coat) looking at the gabbers. A thin old man looking at the ground. Two thin women in pointy glasses, talking. A Lillian Gish-faced woman. A large, solid old woman in a tall hat, furry coat. A skinny woman putting one hand over her face. Three tough-looking, youngish women scowling at the camera, arguing at DAVID.

U.N. ROLL CALL

Nicaragua? *No:* no.
Niger? *Abstention:* abstain.
Nigeria? *Abstention:* abstain.
Norway? *No:* no.
Pakistan? *Yes:* yes.
Panama? *No:* no.
Paraguay? *No:* no.
Peru? *No:* no.
Philippines? *No:* no.

The camera turns the corner of the benches, walks along the next bench row:

An old man in a large tan coat, black hat—sitting on the end of a bench. An old woman in a rhinestone cap, self-consciously turning away from the camera. A short, gabby woman—hair bushing crazily from under a tight cap. A fat woman getting up into the camera. Two skinny, male subway psychos in their late twenties. A dignified, elderly couple looking sideways down the bench. A skeletal old man and a pudgy old man in similar coats and hats. An old woman holding one hand in her lap. A tough old man in a heavy coat (no tie), brown shirt. A heavily made-up woman in a tall cap, red hair; holding a large purse in two hands.

The camera passes:

Two old women talking across their stomachs. A sour woman in sunglasses: a black hat on the back of her head, mock-pearl necklace around her neck. A small old woman, pointing up to the camera. A middle-aged couple—she wears a black-and-white cocked hat. Empty bench space. A tiny old woman hunched over, watching the street. A husky young Puerto Rican with no coat, shirt-sleeved arms folded at his waist. A bedraggled old woman—turning away, pulling back her hair with a puffy hand. A gaunt, proper, gray-haired woman (white scarf hanging in front of her black coat). A heavy old man turned sideways: his fist clenched on the top of the bench. An old woman in a knitted cap, sunglasses. A bulldog old man, his mouth grim. A rat-faced young man: mouth pursed, reading a folded newspaper.

U.N. ROLL CALL

Poland? *Yes:* yes.
Portugal? *Abstain:* abstain.
Romania? *Abstain:* abstain.
Rwanda? *No:* no.
Saudi Arabia? *Yes:* yes.
Senegal? *Abstention:* abstain.
Sierra Leone? *No:* no.

The camera passes:

An old man—sitting forward over his newspaper, hat blocking his face. Empty bench space. A thin, bare-headed old man: sitting up stiffly, with one hand on his knee, lowering his eyes as the camera passes. A stately old woman in a high-collared white coat, her purse held at her waist. A thin, dowagerish woman in a dark coat, pearl necklace; folding her hands. A sharp, little, dark woman and a soft, gray-haired, middle-sized woman leaning together talking. A large, worried lady with a plastic rainscarf on her hair—looking back down the bench over one shoulder. A large, hatless woman with a pompadour of gray hair, and grimace lines deep in her face. A small, roundish woman in a loose coat, pointy plastic glasses. A bench space. A husky, inquisitive man—coat thrown open to his belly—one leg cocked over the other.

U.N. ROLL CALL
Singapore? *Abstain:* abstain.
Somalia? *Yes:* yes.
South Africa? *Abstain:* abstain.
Spain? *Abstain:* abstain.
Sudan? *Yes:* yes.

The camera passes:

A bench space. A thin, weathered man in a dark coat and hat, looking at the ground. A middle-sized "Broadway"-dressed man (thick Mafia sunglasses, tiny-brimmed hat), chewing gum and turning his head to follow the camera. A bench space. Two stooped old women: one straightening herself; the other holding a fist up to her face. A bench space. A runty man in a dirty jacket: his toothless mouth stretched drunkenly closed, palms turning up on his knees. Several bench spaces. A skeletal old man leaning *very close* into the camera, pushing his fingers into his opening mouth. A bench space. A gray-haired, bearish man: leaning back. Several bench spaces. A small, neat, middle-aged man (in dark glasses,

84

dark suit, and dark hat), handkerchief in jacket pocket.

Sweden? *No:* no.
Syria? *Yes:* yes.
Thailand? *Abstain:* abstain.
Togo? *No:* no.
Trinidad and Tobago? *Oui:* yes.
Tunisia? *Abstention:* abstain.

The camera passes:

Several bench spaces. A smiling little woman sitting by her large shopping bag. A small, round man looking up at DAVID passing. A plump woman in a white coat, leaning into the camera. A bench space. A thin woman in a heavy coat: her chin dropping, her eyes averting from the camera. Several bench spaces. A neat, happy young Negro woman, her baby daughter, her sharp husband—all three in smooth, well-fitting white sweaters and jackets. Several bench spaces. Two filthy, ragged, wrinkled bums sleeping: one holding his hands clasped over his chest.

Uganda? *Abstain:* abstain.
Ukrainian Soviet Socialist Republic? *Yes:* yes.
Union of Soviet Socialist Republics? *Yes:* yes.
United Arab Republic? *Yes:* yes.
United Kingdom? *No:* no.
United Republic of Tanzania? *Yes:* yes.
United States? *No:* no.
Upper Volta? *No:* no.
Uraguay? *No:* no.
Venezuela? *No:* no.
Yemen? *Yes:* yes.

Yugoslavia? *Yes:* yes.
Zambia? *Abstain:* abstain.

The camera passes:

A bench space. A man in a dark, rumpled suit—drinking from a flask. A bench space. A short, fat man smoking, one hand thrown up on the bench back. A bench space. Two thin little ladies talking. Four chrome-plated telephone booths in a row at the end of the benches (DAVID is reflected in the chrome-plating as he passes the booths).

U.N. ROLL CALL

Afghanistan? *Yes:* yes.
Albania? Albania?
Algeria? *Oui:* yes.
Argentina? *No:* no.
Australia? *No:* no.
Austria? *No:* no.
and Belgium? *No:* no.

The camera stands:

A pigeon hops in the street at the end of the phone booths.

Fade to black.

Cut to:

The camera is set on a tripod at knee level.

DAVID's room: the paisley-spread bed is close to the camera, the TV set is turned on in the corner. On the TV: an *Outer Limits* episode in which Robert Culp is sent into earth orbit and returns as a large chicken-like creature.

TV

The plan is to send you into orbit as a weather

satellite. The flight has been cleared with the appropriate government agencies. They have no idea, of course, that we're doing this.

DAVID walks into the frame, arms folded across his stomach, pulling on his chin with one hand.

TV

Once in orbit, you will be retro-rocket—

DAVID turns the sound off on the TV, returns to the bed; sits, picks up his telephone. He dials a number. He holds the lavalier microphone against the telephone receiver, leans back toward the camera to check the sound level on the Nagra; sits up—flops back on the bed on one elbow, watching the soundless TV.

(*The phone rings once.*)

DAVID sits upright, turns, pauses.

(*The phone rings again; is answered.*)

DAVID

    H-hello, Penny.

She hangs up the phone.

DAVID drops the microphone tentatively. He swings the phone away from his ear, raps it on the bed—lifts it more forcefully—but then just lays it slackly on the bed. He gets up: swinging his hands, picking at his fingers, walks across the room. Suddenly he stops, stares out the window—not moving for an instant. Then he rushes toward the camera, checking back over his shoulder at what he sees out the window. He steps past the camera.

The camera suddenly tips, moves lopsided across the room to the window.

The bed passes, the windowsill approaches.

At the window, the camera zooms.

S. SCHWARTZ (the-girl-across-the-street) runs down the steps of her apartment building, over the sidewalk. She edges between two parked cars, opens the door to a waiting Volkswagen station wagon, gets in; kisses the driver. The Volkswagen drives off.

The camera pans with the Volkswagen.

Cut to black.

Cut to:

The camera is held directly above DAVID's head by DAVID.

88

(A fish-eye distortion lens is on the camera.) This lens distends the image so that things are very large toward the center of the frame and tiny at the edges; i.e., DAVID seems to have a huge, bulbous head and an ant's body.

DAVID walks along between the Seventy-second Street subway station and the metal-spear fence that runs beside it.

                    DAVID
        Look! Look at this space!

He looks up into the camera: shouting, his hair falling in his eyes.

                    DAVID
        Look at this lens!

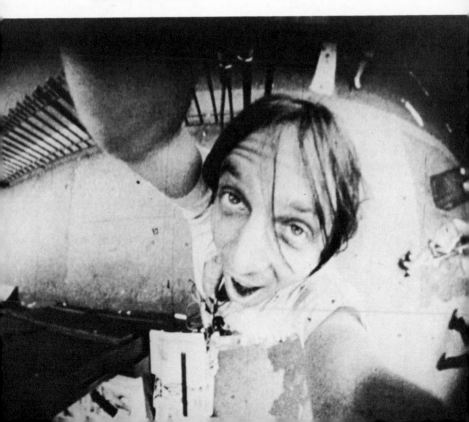

He walks; glances up to the camera; glances behind him; looks up—throws his head back hard to clear the stringy hair from his eyes.

DAVID

> This is great? Look! I just got it! Look at the space! Look: watch! What do I do now?

He starts to walk into the back doors of the station; looks around, walks down beside the station.

DAVID

> I'm going and get in the subway.

He walks into the Seventy-second Street subway crowd.

DAVID

> Watch when I come—I'm gonna come past this. Now, watch: see it? Watch: watch, these people—

DAVID edges past a mother and a little girl through the doors of the subway station into the darkness; turns. He edges back out through the station doors; checking to keep his camera from bumping on the doorjambs.

He walks past the newsstand; stops right beside a newsman who is pointing instructions to his assistant (now self-consciously: when the newsman noticed DAVID, he stopped talking altogether).

DAVID

> Look, look, look, look, look, look.

DAVID follows the newsman and his assistant for a bit.

DAVID walks on: now throws his head back, gasping a bit from the weight of the camera.

The camera shakes; lowers toward DAVID's head.

DAVID reaches up past the lens, wiggling the camera; turns it off.

DAVID

That's it. That's. Okay. Okay.

Cut to black.

Cut to:

The camera faces a pay telephone (the fish-eye lens is still on the camera).

DAVID's hand thumbs two nickels into the phone slot; dials a number, brings the receiver up past the lens.

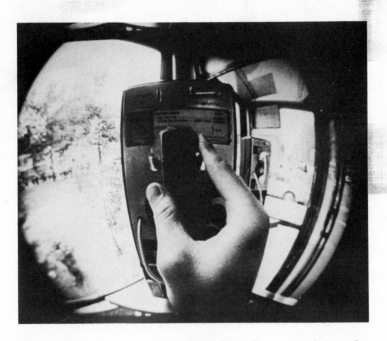

The camera turns in the phone booth, faces down the row of glass-boothed pay phones.

The Nagra sits on the booth shelf, tape running.

(*The phone rings twice.*)

ANSWERING-SERVICE LADY

Yes?

DAVID

Hello, this is David Holzman. Are there any mes-
sages for me?

ANSWERING-SERVICE LADY

Just a minute— Aum— Mr. Holzman?

DAVID

Yes.

ANSWERING-SERVICE LADY

Someone by the name of Penny left a message
for you.

DAVID

Okay.

ANSWERING-SERVICE LADY

Ah-ah-m.

DAVID

Would you read it?

People pass randomly by the booth.

ANSWERING-SERVICE LADY

Ya-yes. She said: Don't call her any more. She
doesn't want you to call her any more. And: hello?

DAVID

Yes. Go on.

ANSWERING-SERVICE LADY

(*Embarrassed*) And she said, Max will be, Max is

coming to your apartment to pick up—aum—her—
clothes.

DAVID
Is that all?

ANSWERING-SERVICE LADY
That's it.

DAVID
Okay, thank you.

The camera turns back in the phone booth to face the
phone.

DAVID's hand reaches; hangs up the phone receiver.

Cut to black.

Cut to:

The camera walks down the sidewalk (the fish-eye lens
is still on the camera).

A few people walk and stand in the street, but the
sidewalk is mainly empty.

The camera stands.

Two policemen squat over a bloody little drunk man
who is flopped against a wall, one shoe off.

RADIO
. . . pleased with the way the war is going, except
in programs that went over the present estimate in
the South Vietnam's government's so-called "Paci-
fication" program.

One policeman notices DAVID; gestures angrily with his
hand for DAVID to get away. The second policeman rises,
turns a heavy face with large sunglasses to DAVID.

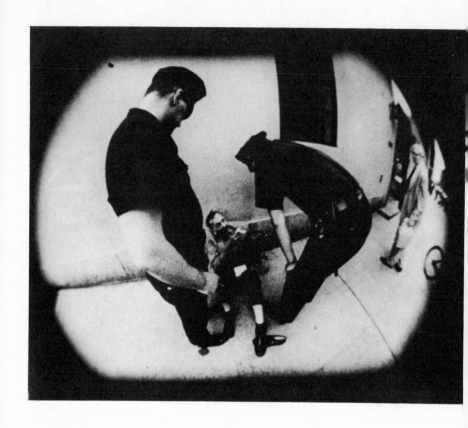

Another unit of American paratroopers has been ambushed in the central highlands of South Vietnam, in the same jungles where another paratroop company was cut to ribbons by the enemy—

The camera turns away a moment; turns back—now moves between the two policemen—now squats to get a close shot of the drunk.

One policeman steps, shoves his ass directly in front of DAVID's camera to block DAVID's shot.

DAVID

And just to keep things straight: this is Thursday, July 20, 1967.

The camera rises, turns away; returns to face the policemen and the drunk, starts to move away.

DAVID

Now I'm sitting at home—waiting for Dear Old Max.

A crowd starts to form around the drunk.

Cut to black.

Cut to:

RADIO

(*Music starts: the electronic anxiety music of the Cream.*)

The camera shoots out DAVID's window.

A young, husky man in a three-piece suit walks down the sidewalk, up the steps, and into DAVID's apartment building.

Cut to black.

Cut to:

The camera faces (at knee level) the short hallway and door to DAVID's apartment.

A photograph of PENNY's head—her hair tossing—is taped to the door. A large poster for Welles's *Touch of Evil* and movie schedules to the cinemathèque, The New Yorker, The Bleecker Street Cinema, The Thalia Theater, The Museum of Modern Art are taped to the wall.

The vested-suit young man opens the door, hesitating

a moment when he sees that he's faced by the camera.
He walks down the hallway shaking his head, smiling
self-consciously.

MAX
Dav-vid.

DAVID
(*Imitating Max*) Dav-vid.

MAX stops; leans one hand against the wall, tilts his
head smugly. He keeps his other hand uncomfortably
flattened against his side.

MAX
You're incredible, you know it?

You're incredible, you know it?

He drops his smirk; purses his lips; crosses DAVID's room.

The camera pans to follow him.

He picks up a white shopping bag from the floor, a dress in a dry-cleaning bag that hangs from the TV; turns, walks out.

The camera pans to follow him.

He stops at the door—looks back as if to say something.

DAVID

Fuck you!

MAX goes out; slams the door.

Cut to black.

Cut to:

The camera faces DAVID's bed (from knee level).

DAVID turns on the camera, sits on the bed—brings both knees up in front of him, leans back. Two windows flank DAVID. He leans into the space made by the small bit of wall between the windows. Directly above DAVID's head, a photograph from *Shane* (Alan Ladd patting Brandon de Wilde on the head for the last time before riding off) is taped to the wall.

DAVID pulls on the lavalier around his neck, drops it against his chest.

DAVID

That's Penny's agent: Max. Call him "Dootch." Fuck yourself, Dootch.

He swings the Nagra earphones in one hand, then flops them on the bed. He kicks out one foot, drops it off the bed; smiles. He lifts the lavalier up to his mouth: waggles the microphone wire, looks down.

DAVID

That fucking vest. He's been wanting to get in her pants. For years.

He picks up the earphones: puts them over one knee, looks down.

DAVID

(*Irish-priest accent*) Yeah—it's a big joke. Let me tell ya, Dootch. It's a big joke!

He stretches a smile, slides the earphones down his ankle, back up to his knee; pulls out one of the earpieces, and pops it against his knee.

He looks above and to the side of the camera silently a moment, tilts his head back.

DAVID

Big ahhha—disappointment.

He looks into the camera—lifts a finger comically—sits up straighter against the wall; puts both his hands on his knees. He looks up to the ceiling silently a moment. He closes his eyes, waggles his fingers; pulls his hands back and rests them at his waist.

DAVID

She's, she's a pretender. You know: the nails, and the—she's, she slobbers.

He lifts the lavalier microphone, looks to the side (smiling), grabs the earphones with both hands; repositions

98

them on his knee—smiles embarrassingly, points to the camera.

DAVID

And the gurgles in her throat. You know. Then: after she's finished, she wants to talk about it.

He looks into the camera silently a moment, his head cocked to the side.

DAVID

She's—Margaret Rutherford.

He shifts the earphones a bit, leans his head back; looks toward his editing table.

He scratches between his eyes, waves a hand forward to the camera.

DAVID

Yeah. Well. Welcome, Dootch. Welcome home.

He drops both hands on his knees, blows some air through his teeth; looks down at his bed. He brings up his lavalier microphone, starts to say something; smiles uncomfortably, licks his lips.

DAVID

(*Bronx accent*) Let me tell ya something. Ay-ah. Since she's been gone, it's been about three days. Ahhaa—getting back to the real stuff now.

He looks to the camera (raises a finger), tilts his head against the wall, looks at the ceiling—nods his head; smiles crookedly at the camera, shifts his eyes a bit.

DAVID

(*Bronx accent*) Mn-masturbation.

99

He brings both hands back to grab the lavalier, ducks his head. He smiles; looks up at the ceiling—waggles his hand, drops it back on his knees.

DAVID

(*Bronx accent*) I mean: sex is sex. You know. If you want, you know: between a man and a woman. *Sex*— But it's never quite like what Norman Mailer writes.

He lifts his arm, stretches it out (looking to the side of the camera), locks both hands: fingers interlocked on one knee.

He twists one shirt sleeve with the other hand; drops the hands together on his knee.

DAVID

(*Irish-priest accent*) But masturbation. You got, you got: you get your contem*pla*tion. This generation sadly lacks contem*pla*tion you get it with mastur*ba*tion.

He's quiet: sticks the thumb and four fingers of one hand up.

DAVID

I mean: you got control. Got the Widow Thumb and her four daughters.

He smiles (closes his eyes), waves one hand in the air, waves both arms a bit—rests both hands on his knees.

DAVID

(*Bronx accent*) You can think up thoughts. You can think of anything. You can think of *pigs*. Think of trains-going-in-tunnels. Think of bagels. I mean, you're not limited to women.

100

He smiles to the side (closes his eyes), brings both hands back to his forehead—stretches them out: drops them back on his knees.

DAVID

I mean when, when ya do: when you do come back to thinking about women. Now!

He looks toward the ceiling, silent.

DAVID

Aaaaah. Ah, you should see.

He grabs the lavalier with one hand—whips the microphone cord up and down a bit—waves a hand; drops the lavalier against his chest, sets his hands on his knees.

DAVID

(*Irish-priest accent*) Dootch. Oh, Dootch. Come back to the True Way, Dootch. Think about. You should see some of the women I think about, Dootch.

He looks silently into the camera for a long moment without moving—his mouth slightly open, front teeth showing. His eyes are blank.

He pulls the earphones off his knee, lays them on the bed; quietly gets up—reaches in front of the camera to turn off the Nagra: looks below the lens, cuts off the camera.

Cut to black.

Cut to:

Night. The camera faces the apartment across the street.

The apartment windows are lit and empty. A dark young man in his shirt sleeves walks up to one of the windows and leans against it: looking down into the street, sipping a can of beer. The girl (s. schwartz) comes up in back of the man; puts her arms around his chest, kisses his ear. The young man turns.

The camera zooms toward the window in two short thrusts.

The young man pulls the girl against him hard; picking

102

her up, her hair flying a little. They twist together, kissing deeper—his hands slide inside her blouse, grabbing at the back straps of her bra. Her hands go up to help him, their mouths still hanging together.

She drops away from him, slowly ending the kiss. Looking over her shoulder at him, she walks back into the rear of the room.

The young man watches her—takes another sip on his beer—moves off after her.

103

The camera zooms back from the window in one smooth move.

The two empty, lit windows stand in the dark.

(*Sound:* DAVID *picks up the phone and dials a number. The phone rings slowly three times.*)

The girl comes into sight in one window, pulling closed a dark bathrobe. She picks up the telephone receiver, leaning her head down to meet it.

> S. SCHWARTZ
>
> Hello?

> DAVID
>
> Sandra?

> S. SCHWARTZ
>
> Who?

> DAVID
>
> Sharon? Sarah?

She shifts tentatively.

> S. SCHWARTZ
>
> No. I think you're calling the wrong number. What number do you want? Hello? Uhmp.

She hangs up.

She moves back away from the window, opening her bathrobe.

(*Sound:* DAVID *hangs up.*)

Cut to black.

Cut to:

The camera faces DAVID's editing table (as at the starting monologue).

Aluminum film cans are stacked on the table. Filmstrips are taped to the edge of the table, the wall beside the table. The open Nagra is on a chair in front of the table. DAVID turns on the camera, stands with his back to it for a moment; sits down in the chair before the editing table.

DAVID
This is Friday. July 21, 1967.

DAVID wears his corduroy bush-jacket, no shirt. He glances up into the camera, looks at the tape recorder; flips the microphone cord around his neck, smiles crookedly—disconnects the microphone, looks at the tape recorder.

DAVID
I got nothing to report.

He drops his smile, looks down at the microphone, up at the camera—hangs the microphone around his neck, frowning.

He looks up at the camera, over at the wall. He lifts the microphone to his mouth—gestures—bites his lip.

DAVID
It's *Fri*day.

He lets the microphone fall against his chest, leans forward in the chair on his elbows (glances up at the camera a split second), looks at the floor quietly. He reaches back—picks up a partly filled fountain Coke glass, sips from it. He looks at the camera, the Coke glass held against his teeth. He looks at the tape recorder—smiles—reaches back on the editing table for a near-empty bottle of Pepsi. He rests the Pepsi on the corner of his chair, looks up into the camera: breaks into a laugh-smile.

105

DAVID

I don't know what you're waiting for.

He takes a deep sip from his Coke glass.

DAVID

I got nothing to say.

He grimaces; pops the plastic lid on the Pepsi, pours some into his glass. He reaches over and taps the volume bar on the Nagra.

DAVID

Unless you want to talk about Vincente Minnelli.

He glances up at the camera—ignores it, takes a short sip of Pepsi.

He sits forward in the chair, glances at the Pepsi bottle— up into the camera (goes poker-face), looks away to the floor; back up at the camera.

DAVID

This is not coming out the way I thought it would. Ahm. See: I thought this would be a film; I thought this would be a film about things.

He smiles; looks up at the camera, over at the tape recorder—leans awkwardly on the arm of the chair, forehead on the fingers of one hand.

He drops his hand to cover his mouth—looks past the camera, closes his eyes—smiles crookedly (looking back into the camera), head tilted to one side.

DAVID

About—The Mystery—of—Things.

He sits back in the chair, looking at his words on the tape recorder. He takes another sip of Pepsi; lifts the

fluted Pepsi bottle up—then extends it toward the camera, holds it there as he looks into the camera a few moments. He pulls the Pepsi bottle back; sets it on the editing table again.

DAVID

I thought that I'd get this stuff on celluloid. And I could, you know.

He gestures unclearly—reaches back and grabs the strip of film that's threaded through the moviescope viewer: rubs it with his thumb, releases it. He glances back at the camera; down toward the Nagra (his fingers hanging on the roof of the viewscope).

DAVID

I could control it. I could run it back and forth, you know. I could: rearrange it until I could see what it meant.

He looks into the camera, pulls his hand toward himself; then back to tap the moviescope, run his fingers over the threading rollers.

DAVID

My Life. On film. I could understand.

He looks at the floor (off to the side), now holding both hands in front of his face. He rests both hands against the Coke glass.

DAVID

I could see what was going on. W-what the on-going thing was. I could make the connections. And I could do what I was supposed to do.

He closes his eyes. He looks up into the camera (smiles), sips from the Coke glass; shakes his head.

DAVID

That's not. That's not what happened.

He sets the Coke glass on the table behind him—slides smiling down in his chair; hands folded in front of him, eyes on the camera.

He blinks; drops his smile; glances at the continually recording Nagra, at the wall. He shifts—cocks one knee up—arches his back—brings a hand to his mouth; looks into the camera, stops moving. He lurches forward: pointing a finger into the lens.

DAVID

Khhhah. *You.* You don't tell me the right things.

You don't show me the right things. You don't show me anything that *means anything*.

He settles back: raises his hands, folds his fingers across one another. He closes his eyes—looks at the ceiling (moves his hands in front of his face)—looks into the camera; grabs the film in the moviescope, pulls it up to his face. He pulls the film closer, stiffens a few frames in his fingers; looks at them, frowning a second.

DAVID
That means anything.

He closes his eyes, drops back his head—starts to gesture, stops—looks into the camera coldly: points at it.

DAVID
Why not?

He retracts his finger. He glances at the ceiling, the camera—drops the filmstrip; starts to get up from the chair. Instead, he reaches and picks up a large yellow pad from the editing table: looks at it, starts to tear a page from it. He sees the running camera again—drops the page, repeats the page-tearing mock-dramatically; leans forward on his knees with the yellow pad, looking at the floor. He glances up at the camera, over at the Nagra; flops the yellow pad back onto the table. He turns and stares closely, quietly into the camera for several moments (mouth drawn shut).

He closes his eyes (half looks away), looks back into the camera; suddenly breaks into a smile, plops back in his chair.

DAVID
What do you want? What do you want?

He starts to get up (half rises), drops back into the

109

edge of his chair; smiles at the camera, looks down at the tape recorder.

His smile goes. He grits his teeth—grimaces, glances at the camera; then above it, then beside it. He clenches one hand into a fist.

> DAVID
>
> I have: *you* have made *me* do things. You haven't told me anything.

He gets up—sticks his hands in his jacket pockets—faces the camera (he's visible on-screen only from the waist to the neck); turns away from the camera; bends to sit down—rises—sits abruptly, smiling.

> DAVID
>
> You have. I have. This is ridiculous. What am I sitting here talking to you? To two machines.

He looks from the camera to the tape recorder; back to the camera, his hair flopping. His smile stiffens a bit. He closes his eyes (grabs his forehead in one hand, covering his eyes).

> DAVID
>
> You have made me do things. Why. What. I don't. Why?

He grimaces; bites his lower lip. He looks up at the side wall; back at the camera; around at the editing table; again at the side wall. He makes a little move toward the camera; looks at it: stops. He closes his eyes; gets up—turns away from the camera, walks out one side of the frame; then walks across and out the other side of the frame, dragging the microphone cord. For several seconds the camera faces only the cluttered editing table, empty chair, Nagra, picture-filled wall.

DAVID
(*Off camera*) What is it?? What do ya want?
What do you want?

The microphone cord pulls back and forth across the
empty chair. A moment; then DAVID returns to the Nagra,
rolling up microphone cord so he can wander more freely.
He walks over to the wall, grits his teeth; jerks a couple
of taped filmstrips down—throws them toward the bed.
He walks in front of the camera, pointing back to the
filmstrips remaining on the wall.

DAVID
You have made me do things—those things.

He walks to one side of the editing table—rips three
filmstrips up from the table, throws them against the
wall—puts his hands in his jacket pockets. He suddenly
sits; smiling embarrassedly (his hand partly covering
his mouth). He waves a hand (shakes his head), his
smile going, glumly looking into the camera.

DAVID
Sh-shh. Wooh. I wouldn't have done those things.

The edge of the film goes white from accidental exposure.

He walks out of the frame. Several moments; then he
half reenters the frame, half gestures to the camera.

DAVID
What do you want?

He leaves the frame.

The camera faces the editing table.

DAVID

What the fuck do ya want?

DAVID breaks back into the frame—slamming one hand on the reels of film on the table (beating on them, clanging them).

DAVID

Why do. Why doesn't this help me? *Why-doesn't-this-help-me?!*

He lurches back out of the frame. For a few more

moments the camera faces the editing table; faces itself in the mirror over the editing table, with the microphone cord jerking in the foreground.

DAVID

What-the-fuck-do-you-want?!!

DAVID rushes back into the frame—up to the camera—cuts it off.

Cut to black.

Silent black screen for a bit.

Cut to:

The camera faces the editing table.

DAVID turns on the camera: faces it, his bare chest and belly showing between the open sides of his jacket.

DAVID

I'm sorry.

He backs up; picks up the microphone cord. He backs up and sits in the editing chair: resting his chin against his hand, looking into the camera. He looks at the floor (half twists his head); straps the lavalier microphone around his neck, watching the camera. He talks to the camera (shaking his head), his arms lying loose on the arms of the chair.

DAVID

Eclair: I'm sorry.

He lifts the lavalier to his mouth, diddles with the Nagra volume bar.

DAVID

Nag: I'm sorry.

He smiles crookedly (mouth half open) at the camera, the Nagra.

DAVID

Twenty-four times a second. *Troot*. This is, this is true.

He looks at the camera—flops his jacket closed, buttons up the jacket—smiling slightly at the camera. He bumps his head against the handle of one take-up reel, glances back at it: rebumps his head.

DAVID

That's true.

He pulls the microphone out from inside his jacket; pulls the film out of the moviescope.

DAVID

It's gotta be true. It is. It's true.

He stares into the camera without moving for a few seconds.

DAVID

It's a deal. I made this deal.

He closes his eyes, leans up; looks into the camera more closely.

DAVID

It's a deal.

He starts to say something; lifts a hand—scratches his nose instead, looks down. He looks at the camera, smiles quickly, looks away.

DAVID

There's no reason to—

He glances into the camera, bends his head forward.

This deal is the reason. This deal *is* the reason. That's the reason.

He presses the microphone against his lips. He glances back at the moviescope; watches the Nagra turning for a few seconds. He starts to move toward the Nagra— turns back toward the camera. He reaches up; gives one last (poker-faced) glance into the lens—turns the camera off.

Cut to black.

Cut to:

Night. The camera walks streets on the Upper West Side.

The camera passes:

A modern apartment-building doorway: a white, blank, empty hallway inside. Two blacks stand in front of the door (watching the camera), one of them uniformed like a policeman-guard.

Cut to black.

Cut to:

The camera passes:

Night. A window: filmy, spotted curtains are unmoving in front of a white-shaded table lamp.

Cut to black.

Cut to:

The camera passes:

Night. Two windows: Venetian blinds lowered, but slats turned open. A television runs in a dark room, a plumpish middle-aged woman turning toward it from her kitchen.

Cut to black.

Cut to:

The camera passes:

Night. A single window: Venetian blinds lowered, slats open.

116

Someone leans on his elbows in the window, watching the street.

Fade to black.

Fade-up:

The camera passes:

Night. Two windows: a handful of people sitting in a kitchen behind thickly barred windows.

The camera pans up:

Three windows: nothing visible in them but the ceiling of a room, the tops of plants.

Fade to black.

Fade-up:

The camera passes:

Night. An old apartment-building hallway: checkerboard floor, bare walls, a large rectangular mirror at the end of the hallway.

The camera pans:

An ornate, 1930's-modern, squarish chandelier in a dark room.

Fade to black.

Fade-up:

The camera passes:

Night. Two windows: behind the filmy curtains, a thick young husband covers his eyes, drops his head back wearily beside a portable, 21-inch TV (its antenna tilted alertly forward). Three plain, thick women in their early

117

thirties hold up a black dress for the approval of another young, flat-topped husband.

Fade to black.

Fade-up:

The camera passes:

Night. A lighted delicatessen's sign behind barred windows. The moon reflected in a window. A darkly lit room, someone reading under a desk lamp (the moon reflected above him in the window glass). A television set running in a dark room.

Cut to black.

Cut to:

The camera stands:

Night. PENNY's apartment window. PENNY, in a cute jumper dress, turns on the TV; walks back into the apartment, smoking.

This is Penny's apartment, there's Penny.

She turns, goes into another room; reenters drinking a Coke.

DAVID

This is the way I ended my shooting adventures on Friday evening. I was halted—

The camera flash-pans:

A skinny policeman walks past a thin tree on the street below PENNY's window, shouting at the camera.

DAVID

—by this man.

The policeman comes toward the camera—glances back toward PENNY's window; turns to the camera, shouting louder. He strides closer to the camera, still shouting. (There is no actual sound of the street.)

DAVID

Hahhm. Ah, watch. (*Laughs.*) Watch him. He's going to hit me now. He's going hit me. Now!

Suddenly the policeman lurches forward with his night stick and shoves it below the camera into DAVID's stomach.

Cut to black.

DAVID

He forced me to go upstairs with him to Penny's apartment. And tell her what I'd been doing. And: he wanted her to press charges. Penny—said: "Forget it." So. Then he went away. And then I went away.

Cut to:

Camera faces an experimental film poster (close-up).

DAVID walks into the frame (only his head and shoulders visible), turns. He has a Band-Aid under his chin. He smiles; looks around, talks comfortably into the camera.

> DAVID
>
> This is Saturday. July 22. There won't be any film shot today. Because I have to go to a funeral in New Jersey. An uncle died. I don't have anything— And I didn't know him. And I don't have anything to say about him. It. The funeral.

He stops, shrugs his eyebrows; walks out beside the camera, cuts it off.

Cut to black.

Hold black.

> DAVID
>
> This is Saturday. The twenty-second of July. I'm in a Duo-Disc recording booth at the corner of Fifty-second and Broadway, making this record for fifty cents. Soon as I finish, I'm going to go over to one of those twenty-five-cent photographing stalls and take some pictures of myself with this—with my Duo-Disc.

Cut to:

The camera faces a 25¢ machine photo of DAVID.

DAVID holds a small white record up in front of his face; looks out from behind the record, a sardonic cast to his eyes.

Cut to black.

DAVID

DAVID
What's happened is that about forty-five minutes ago—

Cut to:

The camera faces a 25¢ machine photo of DAVID.

DAVID holds the record at chest-level, looks down at it quietly.

Cut to black.

DAVID
I got back from the funeral in New Jersey.

Cut to:

The camera faces a 25¢ machine photo of DAVID.

DAVID looks down: flips the record in his fingers, face a little twisted in a smile.

Cut to black.

DAVID

And the apartment was broken into. Everything that you could walk away with and hock in there was taken.

Cut to:

The camera faces a 25¢ machine photo of DAVID.

DAVID looks into the camera (head raised a bit), eyes sad, holding up the record.

Cut to black.

DAVID

Everything: the camera, the still-camera.

Hold black.

Cut to:

The camera faces a 25¢ machine photo of DAVID.

DAVID looks down at the record (smiling slightly), turning the record in his hands.

Cut to black.

> DAVID
>
> The movie camera. The Eclair. Nagra. My Japanese tape recorder. The television set.

Cut to:

The camera faces a 25¢ machine photo of DAVID.

DAVID tugs at the collar of his corduroy jacket, leaning intently forward.

Cut to black.

Hold black.

DAVID

What I came down here to say was that.

Cut to:

The camera faces a 25¢ machine photo of DAVID.

DAVID closes his eyes, holds his hand against his mouth.

Cut to black.

DAVID

This must, this must be the end of the film.

Cut to:

The camera faces a 25¢ machine photo of DAVID.

DAVID brushes his hair back against his head: his eyes closed, head tilted.

Cut to black.

DAVID

This *is* the end of the film. It's finished. It is finished.

Cut to:

The camera faces a 25¢ machine photo of DAVID.

DAVID raises a hand to the camera (in front of his face), frowning.

Cut to black.

Hold black.

DAVID

It's— I wish I could have learned something.

I wish I could have figured something, wish it could have come out.

Cut to:

The camera faces a 25¢ machine photo of DAVID.

DAVID smiles: mouth a little open (dips his head), eyes closed, fingers running on the edge of his record.

                    DAVID
I. Like, like, like Bartleby the Scrivener. Like the Famous Bartleby, I woul—I would have preferred not to have done this. But I did it.

Cut to black.

Hold black.

Cut to:

The camera faces a 25¢ machine photo of DAVID.

DAVID gazes into the camera, quietly holding up the record in both hands, flat.

Fade to black.